MW00987775

Part

Published by June Lundgren

PREFACE

During the years that I have been doing intuitive readings, my clients always ask about my paranormal experiences. They want to know: have I ever seen a ghost? Do angels really exist, and have I seen one? Are all ghosts bad? How can you tell the good ones from the bad? Why do some people see ghosts and others do not? I hope to answer some of those questions in this book. In this book, I will recount some of the paranormal encounters I have experienced in my life. Read on for some interesting thoughts that will help you to better understand the paranormal side of life.

PROLOGUE

What is a paranormal experience? The word "paranormal" is defined by Webster's dictionary as: anything that is beyond the range of normal experience or scientific explanation. This includes phenomena such as telepathy, a medium's abilities, apparitions, Déjà-Vu and telekinesis. I am able to communicate with spirits, angels, animals and other spiritual beings telepathically.

Human beings have often wondered "does everyone have paranormal experiences?" I have found that most people have had a paranormal experience of one type or another in their life. Whether they acknowledge it, or not is entirely up to them. As a psychic medium I can tell you that most people have the ability to sense the paranormal in one way or another. But most of the time we listen to our head and not to our senses. What people fail to understand is that the paranormal and extra-sensory perceptions (ESP) are inextricably linked together.

Some people have dreams that are so real that it is hard for them to separate the dream from reality. It seems like the only time that the spirits on the other side can get through to most of us is in our dreams. It is the only time in the day when our minds are open to receiving messages from the other side. Most of every waking hour is consumed with stress, worry, work and a sundry of electronic devices that are meant to make our lives easier. All of these things keep your mind so busy that you forget to listen to your gut instinct and intuition. Your intuitions, or inner voices as I call them, are the connection to your soul. If you listen to them they will never steer you wrong. If you have a feeling that you shouldn't do something or should do something; don't let your brain talk you out of it or into it, as the case may be. This is a form of paranormal experience because there is no scientific way to verify it.

Almost 80% of the world's population has experienced a paranormal encounter of one type or another in their lifetime. About 60% of these people will write it off to their imagination, fatigue, stress or watching too many horror movies and never give it a second thought. Another 10% will accept the encounter, but will be too terrified to even contemplate the whys or wherefores of the incident. The last group of 10% will be curious, accept what they are seeing and want to explore it further. For some it is the incident that will get them into ghost hunting or exploring the paranormal world. Unfortunately, dealing with the world of the paranormal is not something that is without risk.

Most people who delve into the paranormal are not prepared for the experience and that is where the trouble begins. So, if you are planning on doing some ghost hunting, heed my words of advice. Before you start, learn how to protect yourself physically, mentally and most importantly, spiritually.

Table of Contents

I STILL DO NOT BELIEVE IT

Not everyone believes in the paranormal, or is open to the possibility of another world beyond the physical. There are skeptics who feel that if they cannot touch, see, or hear it, it doesn't exist. My husband Dan is one of those people. He is a wonderful man who calls himself an "agnostic." He believes in a higher power, but does not give it a name.

I think God played a great practical joke when he put us together. Dan is so logical and left-brained that he could not conceive of anything beyond the scope of scientific knowledge. I, on the other hand am so right-brained, emotional and illogical that I sometimes drive him crazy.

I did not tell Dan about my psychic abilities until we had been married a couple of years. After all there was no reason to scare him off. Even after I told him, I don't think he quite believed me, but was willing to humor me.

All that changed one day when my grandmother Edith decided she was going to prove to him that angels and guardians really exist.

On a Saturday night; I went to bed and Dan stayed up to watch a movie. The next morning I was in the kitchen drinking a cup of coffee.

He came in and poured himself a cup of coffee. "So what did you want last night?" he asked.

"What do you mean?"

"You know what I'm talking about," he said frowning at me.

"No, I don't. What are you talking about?"

"About an hour after you went to bed I saw you come out of the bedroom, walk down the hall to Ray's room, check on him, and then stop just short of the living room.

"You looked at me, turned around, walked back down the hall toward the bedroom, and disappeared."

"Well," I replied, "I'll tell you one thing; it wasn't me walking around checking on you. I was asleep, and I didn't get up until morning."

"Yeah, it was you …except you were wearing your glasses."

"Listen, I was not wearing my glasses because I already had my contacts in." I wondered out loud. "What did the glasses I was wearing look like?"

Like most men, Dan does not usually pay attention to things like that. He tried to remember.

"Well, come to think of it, they didn't look like your regular glasses. They were shaped like the old cat's-eye glasses that my mom used to wear."

I got my glasses, which are round, and showed them to him. "'Do these look like the glasses I was wearing?"

"No, not really."

"Well, it wasn't me you saw but someone else."

"No, it had to be you," he insisted, and then paused. "Well, if it wasn't you, who was it?"

I went into the dining room and picked up the picture of my grandmother, who always wore cat's-eye glasses. Handing him the picture, I asked, "Is this the person you saw?"

He looked at the picture intently. "I'm not one hundred percent sure, but it might be the same person."

"This is a picture of my grandmother Edith. She's been dead since 1979. She and I are very similar in looks and stature."

"It sure looks like the person I saw but, it can't be her." He didn't want to believe the evidence of his own eyes.

I smiled. "Grandma says to tell you that because you needed to see to believe, she decided to show herself to you."

Dan continued to refuse to believe what he saw. He put the incident out of his mind until a few months later. He was on his way to the kitchen, walking past the stairs leading down to our family room, when he saw the back of a female figure going down the stairs. Thinking it was me, he shouted out "June?"

I answered from the bedroom. "What?"

"Can you come into the kitchen?"

Sighing, I headed for the kitchen. As I entered Dan asked "Did you just go downstairs a minute ago?"

"No, I was in the bedroom folding the laundry, why?"

He took a deep breath, "I saw her again!"

"Who did you see?" I asked with exaggerated patience.

"Her, you know, your grandmother."

"Oh, is that all? I thought the way you bellowed that something was really wrong."

"Something *is* wrong. Tell her to stop coming around! I do not want to see her."

"Well," I said, "that's your problem. You told me you had to see it to believe it. Now that you've seen her, you still don't believe. When are you going to admit ghosts and angels exist?"

"Okay, I admit she does exist. But that doesn't mean I have to like it when she drops by."

I chuckled in glee. "Well you had better get used to it. They're not going to go away just because you don't like it. In fact, you'll probably be seeing more of them from time to time."

Several months later Dan and I were sitting in the living room late on a Saturday evening watching a movie. All of a sudden I noticed him look up at the opening above my head. On the other side of the opening was the darkened kitchen.

"Ray? Ray?"

"Ray's down stairs." I told him.

"Well then I'm not going to tell you what I saw."

"Alight, what or should I say who, did you see this time?"

"I thought I saw Ray's face in the opening, but I only got a quick look. If he's downstairs then it couldn't have been him."

"What did the face look like?"

"Shoulder length dark reddish hair, pale skin and I think it had blue eyes."

"For someone who only got a quick look you give a pretty detailed description. If the face you saw had blue eyes it couldn't have been Ray. Let me check with my guys to see who dropped by."

"Don't they tell you before they drop by?"

"I always know when one of them leaves, but they don't always tell me when they're up to mischief." I was making the connection with the other side just as my deceased sister, Ann stepped forward.

"Sorry", said Ann. "I couldn't resist; he's such a stubborn cuss that I just had to yank his chain." She said laughing.

"That was not very nice Ann." My great grandmother Hannah chimed in. "Although the look on his face was priceless."

"Hello, are you in there?" Dan asked waiving his hand at me.

"Sorry, it's just as I suspected, my sister, Ann decided to pop in, that's who you saw."

"Tell her not to do that again, and while you're at it tell my mother to stop hitting me on the foot at night. It wakes me up and I have a hard time getting back to sleep again."

"I do it just to make sure he knows I'm around, after all I can't get through to him any other way." His mother chimed in.

"Your mom says it's the only way she can get through to you to let you know she's still around."

"Not true mom, I know you're here when I smell cigarette smoke. No more smacking my foot in the middle of the night, okay?"

Laughing she said, "Okay, okay I promise not to do it again unless there is an emergency."

"She promised not to do it anymore unless it's an emergency."

"Well, she had better not." He said gruffly and let the subject drop.

What I didn't tell him was how she laughed after she promised not to do it again. I figured she would find another way to let him know she was around, even if she had to enlist someone else to help her. And I was right, a few months later she enlisted the help of a couple of our dogs that had crossed over.

It was early on a Monday morning when Dan came staggering out of the bedroom.

"Hey did you open the bedroom door last night and let the dogs on the bed?"

"No, I did not, I didn't notice anything. I must have slept right through it."

"Yeah, you definitely snored through it. Now that I think about it the door wasn't open. It felt like a couple of small dogs jumped on the bed and were walking around then jumped off."

"Just a minute and I'll check with my guys." I connected with Ann. "Tramp and baby girl, wanted to let you know that they are going to come back soon." Tramp and baby girl were two of our dogs who had crossed over.

Since that initial visitation, Dan has had other visits from my family. Each time he is startled by their sudden and unexpected appearance. I believe he needs to see to believe, so therefore he does, grudgingly.

Even though Dan doesn't have the same gifts or beliefs as I do, he has supported me and my gifts in all that I do. This is saying a lot for a modern, logical man. I guess you could say he passed not only my test but the test of those on the other side, too.

GRAVEYARD ENCOUNTER

One Halloween a few years ago my sister-in-law, Linda, called me.

"Hey girl what are you doing for Saturday night?"

"Nothing special that I know of, what's up?" I asked curiously.

"Well, I found out that Oregon City has this guided ghost tour for the next week or so. What do you think about going?"

"Oh yeah," I remembered. "I saw it in the local paper. They take you on a walking tour of homes that are purported to be haunted. You know," I reminded her, "I have to deal with ghosts that show up whenever I go to haunted places."

"Yeah I know, but you can ignore them or put up that protective shield of yours. After all, it's not like we're going to a graveyard."

Linda knew how I felt about cemeteries. I don't frequent them because there can be a lot of spiritual traffic. Ghosts know when a medium is in the vicinity and gravitate to that location. They either want to get a message to someone living or need help crossing over. Everyone wants something, and they're all talking at the same time. It can be overwhelming. My guides taught me how to build a wall of protection so I could block out the incessant chatter.

"It won't keep them all away," I laughed, "but I guess it might be worth the pestering to have a girl's night out."

"That's the spirit." Linda paused. "No pun intended. It starts at 8 pm. They have several tours, one right after the other, so if we're late we can wait for the next one. It costs four dollars and lasts around an hour."

"Okay, I'll pick you up; make sure you get an address."

"I'll get everything, she said, "See you Saturday night."

I hung up the phone.

"What have I agreed to? I thought. "Oh well, I don't get to see her that often." and I resigned myself to the trip.

Saturday night arrived dry, clear, and cold. I picked up Linda and drove to the Carnegie Library building to await the start of the tour. People were milling around talking about it. We waited over fifteen minutes for someone to announce the next one.

"I wonder if we're in the right place," I said, looking around. "I haven't seen anyone who looks like a tour guide. Maybe we should ask inside to see if they know where we are supposed to pick up the tour."

"I think you're right. People are talking about a ghost tour but I don't know if it's the one we want. Let's go inside and see what we can find out."

We climbed the stairs to the building, entered the warm foyer, and headed through double doors into a large room filled with books and statues. There was an older woman at a desk on the far side. We made a bee line for it.

"Excuse me," I asked, "can you tell me where we wait for the ghost tour?"

"Certainly," the woman obliged. "All you need to do is wait on the sidewalk in front of the stairs and a mini bus will be there in a few minutes. Just get on board when the others get off."

I thanked her, and we turned to head for the door.

"Well," Linda said, "we're in the right place, but I could have sworn that it was a walking tour. Maybe the bus takes us to the area and that's where the tour starts."

"I don't see anyone out there leading people around. Okay, we'll wait."

We talked for another five minutes and the mini bus finally arrived. Several people got off, and we climbed on board. We sat down and waited for the bus to fill up. Once full, the driver made an announcement over the microphone.

"Welcome to the Pioneer Cemetery Haunted Ghost Tour."

Linda and I looked at each other in surprise and laughed. People turned to look at us but we couldn't help ourselves

"I guess I'm going to a graveyard whether I want to or not!" I groaned.

"It seems like someone wants you to go to the cemetery tonight. I wonder what they want." Oh well, could be worse."

"And just how could it be worse than a deserted *old pioneer* graveyard at night? You do realize that this cemetery is over a hundred years old and the last person to be buried here was in the early 1900's," I asked her.

"We could be at Gettysburg," she said earnestly, "or in the middle of Egypt's Valley of the Kings. You'd really have your work cut out for you there!"

I turned to her, and we burst out laughing again "You're right," I admitted. "Of course, you're right that would be much worse."

"I told you." She said with a grin." Do you think your protective shield will stave off the masses?"

"I'm not sure maybe I need to reinforce it a little more."

Closing my eyes, I extended the range of my field out from one foot to three.

"Are you done yet, because I'm sure we're getting close?"

She had no more than finished her sentence when the bus suddenly stopped. Only then did we notice that we had arrived at the cemetery. Everyone was beginning to move towards the door to get off. We followed.

As we stepped off the bus, I felt spirits approaching. Ghosts in graveyards know when open people are going to be visiting. We are like a light in the darkness. They show up to see if we'll listen to them.

"Drat, I thought, my protective shield would give me some time to prepare myself for the onslaught." I mumbled.

"How many are spirits are there; five or ten? Linda asked smiling in excitement.

"Try thirty or forty. And why are you so darn happy about it?"

"I am so happy because I get to see you work. Not that I can actually see anything. It's just so exciting and mysterious and it's not like I get to see these things all the time."

"Whatever," I said. "Let's pretend we're checking markers. People get a nervous when they see me doing this kind of thing, and I don't want to cause a scene."

"We walked as far away from the others as we could without being obvious.

"So how does it work?" Linda asked. "Am I in the way? Is there someone standing next to me?"

"You can stand where you are. All you have to do is be quiet. I have to clear my mind and talk to them telepathically."

Closing my eyes, I opened myself to the spirits. There were all manner of ghosts around me. Some were still locked in their death state, appearing how they looked at the moment of their death. This occurs in traumatic deaths – a car crash, a fall, or gunshot. Others were confused and searching for someone to help them.

I have to make ghosts realize that I will not put up with chaos. Once they realize they won't get help until they are quiet, they tend to settle down. I usually put them together in two groups – one for those who want help crossing over or delivering messages, the second for those who do not know they are dead.

"Those of you, who don't know where you are, raise your hands."

Over half of them raised their hands.

"How many of you want to get a message to someone?"

All but three raised their hands.

"Those of you who have other issues go over and stand by Linda"

The last three went to stand next to her.

"Hey, it's really gotten cold over here," Linda complained as she hugged her jacket closer to her body.

I grinned at her in the darkness.

Straining her eyes she asked, "Are you smiling? Okay what did you do to me? Whatever it is I don't like it. Are they standing by me?" she asked nervously.

"Don't worry there's only three standing by you. The rest are standing by me. You said it would be exciting so I figured you might want to get in on the action."

"Ha ha, very funny just get on with it will you, before I freeze to death."

"Alright, alright, you're just no fun." I said laughing at her.

I turned to the group in front of me.

"Okay, listen up," I commanded. "Everyone stop talking. I need to tell you something very important."

"Here it is in a nutshell; you are all dead!"

Everyone started talking again, louder this time.

"Quiet down so you can hear me. I know it's a shock to you but you must have wondered why no one could see or hear you. It's not a dream or a nightmare. It's real!"

Someone shouted, "This is just great, my stock portfolio is worthless now."

The comment triggered an onslaught of comments and questions. I listened to the questions and comments for a few moments, and then shouted.

"Knock it off everyone. I know you all have questions and I'll do my best to answer them. If you just listen to what I have to say a lot of them will be answered."

After a moment or two they were quiet again.

"Now I'm sure you want to know what's going to happen next, where you're loved ones are and how to get there."

Everyone murmured their agreement.

"Okay, all you have to do is listen and do what I tell you and you'll all get there. Is everyone ready to start?"

They all nodded yes.

"I want you to look around you and see if you can find a light. It may be very small. If you see it start heading toward it. The closer you get the larger it will become. As you walk toward it, think of your loved ones, and they will come and take you with them."

Cries of happiness and exclamations about loved ones filled my head, until the last of the spirits passed. Tears of happiness ran down my cheeks and I wiped them away.

I turned to the last three souls to access their conditions. Two of them remained in their death state. What I mean is they appear how they looked at the moment of their death. This occurs when the person has had a traumatic death, car crash, fall, or gunshot.

I motioned them over to where I was standing.

"What's happening?" Linda wanted to know. "I'm warmer now. Are they gone yet?"

"They're over here with me and there's only three left so it won't take long."

"You are dead," I told the three. "Some of you are still in your death state and cannot find your physical body to verify this."

They all nodded.

"All you need to know is that it is true, you are dead, and you can cross into the light if you are ready. Do you have any questions or concerns about crossing over?"

"What if you were not a good person in life?" an older woman asked.

"I overcharged my clients and took a piece of the profit for myself," confessed the man in a rumpled suit wearing glasses and carrying a briefcase.

"I left my wife and child and was rushing to meet my mistress when the carriage I was driving turned over," said the man who looked like he died in the 1800's. "Can I be forgiven for committing adultery?"

"I know you are afraid of judgment or not being let into heaven," I reassured them, "but you don't have to worry as long as you ask for His forgiveness. He will accept you into the light. You all have done things you need to answer for. You might have to spend some time in limbo. But at least you will be with your loved ones."

One by one they found the light, and slowly, hesitantly, made their way toward it, eventually disappearing completely.

Turning to Linda I said, "They're gone now. All of them made the transition to the other side."

"Are they gone?" Linda asked, not hearing me.

"Yes they all crossed. I'm just glad that I didn't have to deal with any troublemakers this time."

The bus started to fill up as the tour returned. "We'd better get a seat," I alerted Linda. "Maybe we can do the walking tour another time."

"Yeah, I'm with you there," she said. "Enough ghost adventures for one night, I think it is time to go home and get warm."

"At least we're not taking any spirit attachments home with us!" I laughed. Linda turned serious fast.

"Are you telling me that ghosts can attach themselves to us and follow us home? You didn't say anything about that being a possibility!"

"You never asked, so I figured I wouldn't worry you by mentioning it. Besides I'm with you and you're protected by my protective shield, so it was never really an issue."

"Alright, but next time warn me, will you?"

FOOTSTEPS IN THE HOUSE

Shortly after my husband and I were married we were looking for a house. A friend of ours told us about a place down the block from where he lived. It was perfect for us, so we bought it and moved in.

About a year later my husband noticed that the back bedroom felt cold sometimes. It didn't all the time, just once in a while. He didn't mention it to me for some time. I began to hear what sounded like footsteps on a hardwood floor. But we didn't have hardwood floors, ours were carpeted and there was no one home but me and the dogs. The footsteps only occurred once in a while. I could never predict when it would occur.

My husband slept in the back bedroom when he came home from work. He worked nights, I worked days and I was pregnant.

We were having breakfast one weekend when my husband Dan brought up the coldness in the back bedroom.

"Hey, have you noticed how cold the back bedroom is? I wonder if there's a blockage in the vent line."

"Yeah, I've noticed it does feel cold some times."
I didn't want to bring up the fact that I thought it
was a ghost. I hadn't told him yet that I was a
psychic medium.

"Well, if it continues I'll have to run something
through the line to see if there's a block."

"Okay, let's monitor it for a little while so we can
tell if we need to do that."

"Alright. I'll try to remember to make a note of it
when it happens." Since he didn't mention
anything about the footsteps, neither did I.

One day after I got home from work, I went to
the back bedroom and sat down on the bed.
Opening myself up to the other side I could
sense a presence, but it wouldn't come forward.

"Are you with me or are you just an echo of
what was? Come forward and let me know what
you want."

At first everything was quiet. Then the bed
started to shake. The movement of the bed
surprised me for a moment for two. I waited
silently for a telepathic response. For the next
several minutes the room was oddly silent. The
dogs that never strayed very far from my side
were pacing restlessly. I knew whatever was
there was not very far away because I could feel
the nervousness of the dogs.

"Who are you and what do you want?" I asked,
again no response. "Did you die here?"

I was growing impatient with this entity. I knew it was there but was choosing not to respond. It was growing late and I was tired of the lack of communication. Being nice was getting me nowhere with this spirit. It was time to take charge, so I decided to get tough and provoke it. I got up from the bed and shouted, "Listen to me you half-baked entity. I know you're there and that you come and go all the time. I am tired of putting up with you. You need to tell me what you want or I am going to banish you from the physical world and be done with it!"

Suddenly the lights started to flicker and it got even colder in the room. "I see you're listening. That's a step in the right direction. Now tell me who are you and what you want."

I received a telepathic response.

"My name is Ed, and I used to live down the street."

"Okay, so what are you doing here? Do you need my help?"

"I came here hoping to make contact with you. They told me you could help me."

"Who told you I could help you?" I asked.

"My spirit guardians, Hannah, and Ann said I could help you."

"How can I help you? Do you have a message for someone?"

"I need you to give a message to your friend Dennis."

"Oh, I get it. You're the old owner who died in his house. He told me he bought it from a woman whose husband died."

"Yes, I've been trying to get through to him for the past few months and he won't listen to me. He's very stubborn and if he doesn't listen it could cost him his home."

"If I give him your message will you stop visiting me and cross over?"

"Yes, I promise. Just give him this message. Tell him that I did some of the wiring in his house and that the wiring in the attic is not the right kind and it is going to cause a fire up there. He needs to replace it right away. There's no time to waste. I don't want to be the cause of someone dying. I couldn't rest knowing I caused their death." He signed heavily.

"Okay, I'll let him know tonight so he can get started on it right away."

"Thank you for all your help, Hannah was right, you are willing to help us." Then he left.

I noticed the room immediately became warmer and lighter. The dogs who had left the room when the ghost came in wandered back into the bedroom.

Reaching down I gave each of them a reassuring ear rub. "It is ok guys, the ghost is gone and you don't have to worry about him coming back anytime soon."

Heading for the living room I grabbed the phone and dialed Dennis's number. He answered almost immediately.

"Hey, it's me. You need to sit down and listen to me. I have a very important message for you." I proceeded to relay the events which, had just unfolded in the bedroom. After I was through, he said "Wow, no kidding, I guess I had better take care of the wiring as soon as I can. Thanks for giving me the heads-up. Hopefully he'll stop bugging you now."

A few weeks later, my husband and I were watching a program on television one evening when he said, "You know, I haven't noticed the bedroom being cold anymore. It must have been something that got caught in the vent has passed."

"Yeah, I noticed that too. I'm glad we didn't have to run something down it. It would have been a pretty messy job." I said, making a face at him.

"I'm really going to have to tell him about my gift," I thought, "but first I need to tell him he's going to be a dad." After all, I was starting to show, and I thought one shock at a time was all he could handle. I thought "I guess I'll wait for a while to spring my abilities on him, after all he doesn't believe in anything paranormal, yet."

GHOSTS ARE PEOPLE TOO

Ghosts were people at one time. They had families, raised children, and watched their loved ones die. They are as unpredictable in death as they were in life. A ghost's personality is pretty much what it was when they were alive. If they were nasty in life, then they are nasty in death. They have feelings and emotions just like the rest of us.

About ten years ago I was sitting in my living room around midnight, watching TV. I had been busy most of the day running errands and shopping. A female ghost had been bugging me most of the day.

"You need to help me. I know you can hear me. Why don't you answer me?" she all but shouted at me.

"Alright, alright, I hear you. You're going to have to wait until later when I have a few minutes to talk." I told her.

"Why do I have to wait, why can't you help me now?"

"Because I'm busy and because you need to wait until I'm ready or not at all."

Finally I got some free time after my husband and son had gone to bed.

Closing my eyes I cleared my mind and spoke to her.

"Alright you, let's get to this."

When I opened my eyes I found her standing in front of me. When I communicate with ghosts I speak telepathically. It's easier for them, and it doesn't make me look like a crazy person talking to herself.

"So what is so important that you had to keep bothering me all day?" I asked.

"I have to get a message to my son right away, it's very important," she answered.

"Ok, I understand that you want to get a message to him, but why couldn't you have gone through my guides? They would have made sure that I got your message."

"It's a very important message and I needed to make sure he gets it. It's not that I don't trust them, but I would feel better knowing that I did all I could to get the message to him." She explained to me.

I empathized with her, being a mother myself.

"What is your name and what year did you die? I knew for certain by her dress that she died a long time ago, and her son would have been dead for many years. But I needed to get more information in order to help her

She thought about my question for some time.

"My name is Susan and I'm pretty sure it was 1801 when I died."

"How long have you been looking for someone to help you?"

"Oh, not very long, seems like yesterday." She smiled hesitantly.

I sighed heavily, trying not to give away my thoughts. Unfortunately, some ghosts do not seem to notice the passage of time.

"How did you die?"

"It was right after my son was born. I got real sick. I slept a lot because of the fever. When I fell asleep the last time it was a long time before I woke up. When I did wake up I couldn't find my baby boy or my husband. I got kind of confused after that. I tried talking to people, but no one seemed to be able to hear me. That's when I guessed that I must have died."

"Well, how did you find me?" I wondered. "I don't usually have anyone follow me home. I may be a medium, but I am not on duty 24/7."

"What's a medium?" she wanted to know.

"A medium is someone who can speak to, and hear, the dead."

"Do you mean a witch? Are you a witch?" she asked in horror.

"No, I am not a witch! It's a gift that God gave all the women in my family. Some call us seers or say we have the "sight." I said, trying to make her understand in terms that would equate to her time frame.

"Oh, I understand. My grandma had a gift of healing. Some said she was a witch, but I didn't believe them. She said God taught her how to heal with herbs."

I dreaded having to tell her that her son was dead. She had waited so long to find someone who could hear her. "Susan, how long do you think you were asleep? Do you know what year it is?" I asked gently.

"I don't know how long I slept before I woke up. I don't know what year it is. Has it been more than ten years?" she asked fearfully.

"Susan, it has been over two-hundred years since you died." I said gently.

I closed off communication for a few minutes so she could process the information.

"You're wrong. It can't be that long. I tell you it can't be more than a year or two at the most," she said, panic filling her voice.

"I'm not wrong. Look around." I spread my arms wide to encompass the room.

She turned and really looked, at her surroundings.

"It's 2005, Susan, and your children and great-grandchildren have been dead for a long time. I am so sorry you had to find out this way. If you had just crossed over completely you would have seen them grow up."

"You're lying," she shouted angrily. I can't have been asleep that long. It's not true."

"All you have to do is look for the light and walk into it. You'll find your son and husband there."

I could tell she still had doubts and was mad at me for not listening to her sooner. She gave me a glaring look and proceeded to walk straight through me. The impact of her hitting me sent my rocker-recliner swinging wildly and I went numb, cold and tingly all over. Boy, do I hate that feeling. It had happened to me several years before.

Most ghosts just want to be left alone. So you see, ghosts are people, too. And pretty much the same as when they were alive. When word spreads about a place being haunted, people come from everywhere to poke and prod the spirits, and they become a sideshow with no peace. When people bug them too much ghosts get irritated and annoyed. They have a way of getting back at the living when they get fed up with us bothering them. They can push, shove, hit, slap or pull your hair.

NOW YOU SEE IT, NOW YOU DON'T

There have been documented occurrences of angels protecting people from harm when by rights that person should have died. They have been known to keep a car, plane or train from its intended trip by causing a delay due to engine trouble or mechanical/electrical issues that delay their departure. In 1998, I got to see angelic intervention first-hand.

The morning started off like any other, rushing to get ready for work and get my eight-year-old son ready for school. We were about to leave, I reached to pick up my purse, but it felt light. I always carried a heavy organizer in my purse, so it usually weighed 3 to 4 pounds. Something was wrong, looking inside I could see the organizer wasn't there.

"Ray have you seen my organizer?" I asked my son.

"No, isn't it in your purse?"

"No, it's not there, and I didn't take it out."

"Well I didn't touch it," he said.

"We need to start looking; my driver's license is in the organizer."

We spent the next 10 minutes searching everywhere we thought it might be with no luck. I was going to be late for work and Ray was going to be late for school.

"I'll just have to take a chance and drive without it this morning," I told him.

As I picked up my purse, I realized it was heavy again. Looking inside, I saw the organizer back in my purse.

"Ray, it's back in my purse. Did you put it there?"

"No, Mom I didn't find it. I was still looking for it." We looked at each other knowingly and headed out the door. I didn't have time to find out the reason for the organizer's mysterious disappearance.

I was certain my older sister Ann, who is one of my guides, had something to do with the disappearance.

After getting home from work I made dinner. After dinner was over I sat down in my meditation room and connected to the other side.

"Ann, you took the organizer didn't you?"

"Well it's like this", she said calmly. "We couldn't just come right out as say, 'Hey, June Ann I don't think you should leave right now. If you do, you are going to be involved in an accident.'"

"Well, why not? After all, you're supposed to be protecting me, aren't you?"

"It's not as simple as that. There are laws and rules that we as guides and guardians have to abide by. One of the rules is that we cannot tell you of an accident or when you are going to die. The only way we could work around that particular rule was to delay your departure."

"You could have just said 'be careful driving or be careful on your way to work."

"No, that would be just like telling you about the accident. Instead we chose to delay your departure, thereby keeping us and you out of trouble. We've been known to bend the rules a little from time to time if the need should arise."

I looked at her with a raised eyebrow, "Now, you're just splitting hairs, and I think you're doing more than bending the rules a little, if you ask me. I wonder if Michael knows how you bend the rules."

"Where do you think we learned how to bend them?" She said smiling smugly at me and disappeared.

This was the first of several heavenly rules and laws I would see them bend in years to come. They also have angels that enforce those rules and laws. If it is a minor infraction, then those angels under the Archangels take care of the discipline. If the soul breaks a major law then this is where the avenging angels come in to play. They dispense punishment befitting the situation.

This left me wondering just what they were not telling me. I didn't know it at the time, but they knew I was an old soul. Just how old, I was to discover several years later. I was given a personal mission by God, which would also be revealed at a later point in my life. I was only to find out later that my soul was one of the first to make the transition of physical body to pure energy. Before we incarnated into this physical world we had lived other physical lives on another world. It took many thousands of years for us to evolve into beings of pure energy.

THE PUSHY GHOST

Can ghosts hurt you? Some people are under the misguided belief that they can't. But if ghosts are powerful enough, they can scratch, trip, slap, shove or lift you, as well as throw objects at you. It was around 5:30 in the morning, I was on my way down to the barn to feed the cows and barn cats. I was almost to the barn when suddenly both feet went out from under me and I fell in the wet, muddy grass. Swearing I picked myself up off the ground and made my way into the barn. I didn't think much of it at the time. I just figured the grass was wet and muddy so I slipped.

About a month passed with no incident. Then one morning I was once again walking down to the barn. As I reached the wet grass I was careful not walk too fast to keep from slipping. I made it halfway to the barn when my left foot slipped and I fell on my leg.

Entering the house my husband looked at me and asked, "What happened, did you fall again?"

"Isn't that what it looks like?"

"Did you hurt yourself, are you ok?"

"My legs sore but it'll be okay. Maybe it's the smooth soles on the slippers. I think I need to wear the boots instead, they have a better tread." I was beginning to have my suspicions that there was something more to it than me being clumsy. Everything went smoothly for a couple of months. It was early spring and as I stepped outside I felt a difference in the air. The air seemed to be heavier, in my experience it was a sure sign of spirit activity. Opening myself up I knew there was a negative presence close by. I took a moment to reinforce my white light protection. I carefully made my way down to the barn and fed the animals.

I started back to the house keeping my senses open for the entity that I felt was still close by. I was almost at the house when the air suddenly became very cold. I stopped looking around for the source of the unexpected coldness. I could sense its presence but didn't realize just how close it was. Suddenly I felt a shove from behind and fell to the ground swearing.

That's when I heard the laughter, not nice laughter but dark and sinister-sounding.

"Oh yeah, we'll see who has the last laugh." I said to the entity. I was thoroughly mad. Picking myself up off the ground I stood silently infusing even more white light energy into my protective energy field.

"How could you have been as stupid as to not see what was happening before this?" I muttered to myself.

I had only myself to blame. I was keeping myself closed psychically and I kept putting off laying down a line of protection around my property. Things seemed to be quiet, so I assumed everything would be okay until I could put the protection in place. I should have known better than to leave myself, my family and my property unprotected against the dark ones.

The following day was Saturday; I got up early to prepare a container of blessed black salt and to make my stand against the negative. I tuned in to the entity and could feel it waiting outside, it dared not enter my home as it was protected by a blessed cross. Tuning in on it I was able to find out what it was up to. It was under the misguided impression that I would be unable to do anything to stop it from tormenting me. I smiled to myself, obviously it was unable to read my mind or it would not still be hanging around.

Opening myself up further, I made connection with the angelic realm, and filled myself with the power and protection of the white light of God. I could feel its power entering my body, warming and energizing me. Once I finished I connected with Michael.

"Hey Michael can you just sort of standby if I need you while I'm dealing with this jerk?"

"Sure no problem, I won't show myself unless you need me."

"Okay, I had better get to it, the sun is coming up."

Bracing myself I headed out into the middle of my hay field to make my stand. Sitting down I called the entity to me.

"Hey you, stupid, who do you think you are to push me around? Do you really think you can mess with me and not pay the price?"

I heard an evil sounding laugh coming from somewhere to my left. "You would challenge me? You are an insignificant human nothing more."

I laughed in amusement, "You can't fool me, I know what you are. You're nothing more than a two bit ghost. You would try to make me believe that you are something you're not. I know that you had human form once. So that rules out you being a demon, like you would have me believe. I'll agree that you're negative, now let's look a little deeper and see who you really were." I knew that there was something it was hiding. Probing deeper, I could see the echoes of a life filled with violence and pain. I got the sense of the 1920's, the gangster era. This entity was a male who fit the profile of a killer for hire.

"So you were a killer for hire, but I sense there was something deeper to it than just money or control." Then as if a door opened I could see that he actually enjoyed killing. He believed that he could play God and get away with it.

"No wonder you can't rest, you're still haunted by the murders you committed."

"No, they deserved to die; they were weak, not worthy of living."

"Who are you to play God? You're still trying to harm people by eliciting fear in them. But this time you picked on the wrong person." I warned him.

"You can't do anything to stop me!"

"You like to mess with people's minds, always trying to control how they see you. Well two can play that game, let me show you who I am!" Reaching out with my while light energy I held him in place.

"Let me go, you can't do this to me."

"How does it feel to be afraid? Wait I'm not done yet, you should be afraid, very afraid. Michael it's time for you to take out the trash." Archangel Michael grabbed the entity and they disappeared.

The sun was pretty well up, gathering my container of black salt and my white sage I headed to the far corner of the field and laid down the line of protection. Once the circle was complete, I buried a blessed cross at the point of closure.

"Stupid ghost!" said a voice behind me.
"He was just too stupid to realize who he was messing with."
"Oh well, he soon learned that you shouldn't mess with a light worker. Now he pays the price for all the pain he's caused others. And by the way you were conspicuously absent during all of this."
"God said this was something that you had to face on your own. He said that you needed to understand that you had the power through Him to confront evil in any form and defeat it."
"God gave me another test? Will these tests ever end?"
"I think you will always have tests, June Ann. It is part of not only serving God, but also it is also a confidence builder for you.
From that day forward, I never had another problem with any ghost or negative entity around my home or property.

A MATCH MADE IN HEAVEN

It was 1987 and I had just come out of a two-year relationship, which left me feeling bitter about men in general, and I was very depressed. The last thing I wanted was another relationship; I just wanted to be by myself for a while. For months after my breakup a close friend of mine, Dennis, was always trying to fix me up with different guys. He felt guilty because the person I broke up with was a friend of his.

"Listen, I do not need another problem in my life, which is what another guy is."

"Come on, you've got to get out more often, you can't spend your life staying at home." He insisted.

"I get out, I go to work every day and on the weekends I spend time with my four legged children. I get to spend some quality time with them."

"I'm sorry Ted turned out to be such a jerk. You are better off without him; you don't need people like that in your life."

"I agree but it's the betrayal that bothers me the most. It shows that he had no respect for me and I won't tolerate that."

"You know I'm not going to give up on this. I have a real nice guy I think you should meet. I think that he's real lonely. He's a little older than you and set in his ways, but he stable and not a jerk."

"Okay, okay, if it'll shut you up I'll go out with this guy. But don't blame me if we don't get on." I reluctantly let him give my phone number to his friend.

A couple of days later on a Friday night my phone rang.

"Hello."

"Is this June?"

"Yes, who's this?"

"My name is Dan and Dennis asked me to give you a call."

"Oh yeah, he said a friend of his would be calling." We talked for a few minutes and he seemed nice enough.

"Would you like to go out for coffee this weekend?" He asked.

"No, I can't, I'm busy this weekend." Even though, I would not be busy, and that wasn't true.

"Oh, Okay." He said sounding disappointed. I've always been a soft touch when it comes to hurting people's feelings so I relented

"Do you like fishing?" I asked him.

"Yes I do."

"How about we go fishing next Saturday? You can pick me up at 5:30 and we'll go."

"Great, I'll be there." He said.

"Don't you want my address?" I asked him.

"Oh yeah, let me get some paper." He said.

I could tell he was excited that I had agreed to go out. The following Saturday he arrived a little before 5:30. I had dressed in my usual fishing attire, no makeup, combat boots, my old fatigue pants and a well-worn t-shirt. I figured that if he was going to go out with me he should see me at my worst. He could either accept me at my worst or he could get out and not let the screen door hit him on the way out. He was shorter than most of the men I dated, and older, by 14 years I found out later.

My guides and guardians were not saying much at this point, which was odd for them, but I figured they would let me know when they had something to say. I could sense a spirit around him but she wasn't saying anything, so I ignored her. I opened the front door and came out to meet him, pole in hand.

"Hi, I'm Dan." He said

"I know, can we go to Dunkin donuts and get some coffee, I need coffee." I said.

"Sure no problem, is one around here?"

"Yeah, there's one a few blocks away." I said, and gave him directions.

With coffee in hand we started to head out of town.

"Where do you want to go?" He asked.

"I think we should go up the Clackamas River and rent a small boat for a few hours. What do you think?"

"Yeah, that's fine."

So we headed out to Promontory where they rented boats by the hour. I chose an eight foot aluminum boat with a trolling motor which I had rented several times before. We spent the next few hours fishing and talking. After we got back to the dock and had turned the boat in, he told me that he didn't know how to swim.

"What, are you crazy? What if the boat had tipped over? I wouldn't have been able to save you with all this gear on!" I all but shouted at him. He just smiled at me.

'Well it didn't tip over did it?" He said.

I just shook my head at him and headed for the truck. Over the course of the next few months we went out off and on. I was not enamored of him, but he sort of grew on me. He was good company and made me laugh, which was something I had not done for some time. During that time I found out that he referred to himself as agnostic. He was very left brained and logical; if you couldn't touch, feel or see it, then it didn't exist. Wow, the exact opposite of me! I didn't tell him about my gifts, I figured he would probably think I was crazy.

About four months after we met I was involved in a motorcycle accident. I was riding my bike when a woman ran a red light and hit me. Fortunately it wasn't serious, a concussion and a right arm fracture. My next door neighbor at the time, Carola and I, were best friends. When I was in the ER her phone number was the only one I could recall. My mother has just changed her phone number and I didn't know it by heart. She got my mother's phone number from my house and called her to let her know I was in the hospital. She had a set of my house keys and was at my house when Dan stopped by.

As Dan pulled up in front of the house Carola came out of the door.

"Hey Carola is June home?" he asked.

"No I just got a call from her; she's at Adventist hospital in the emergency room."

"What happened, is she okay?"

"Someone hit her while she was riding her motorcycle. She must be okay otherwise she wouldn't have been able to have called me."

"I'm going over there now; I'll call you and let you know what's going on." He assured her as he left for the hospital.

I spent 2 days in the hospital and Dan picked me up when it was time for me to go home. On the way home he asked me about going out to dinner.

"How about stopping for some dinner?

"Not tonight, I want to get home to the dogs, I'm going through dog withdrawal."

"What about tomorrow night then?"

"Okay, but I need to get home early; I have to go back to work tomorrow."

The next night after dinner we got into his truck and he pulled a small box out of his pocket. I opened the box hoping it wasn't what I thought it was. When I opened it a yellow gold wedding set was nestled inside.

I snapped the lid shut handed it back to him and said the first thing that came to mind. "What did you want to go and do that for!"

"I want to marry you, that is why." He said quietly.

I paused, "Well I can't wear yellow gold, and I'm allergic to it. You're going to have to return this and get your money back."

"Okay, I can do that." He said eagerly.

What I didn't tell him was that the ring he chose was ugly. I never did say yes, just phoned him one night and said, "If we're going to get married we have a few things to talk about. I need some space. I just got out of one disastrous relationship and don't want to make another mistake." I made him wait almost a year before we got married.

Shortly before our marriage my great-grandmother Hannah, one of my guardians, came to me.

"I have something important to tell you." She said.

"And what might that be?" I asked her. I was only half listening to her because I was right in the middle of one of my favorite TV shows.

"You really need to listen to me."

"Can't it wait until my show is over?" I asked impatiently.

"No, we need to talk now." She said and the TV turned off.

"Okay, okay, so what's so terribly important that it couldn't wait until the show was over?" I asked

"I have something to tell you and I don't think you're going to be happy about it."

"Okay, so what's wrong?" I said eyeing her suspiciously.

"You know that we love you and only want what's best for you, right?"

"Yes, I love you, too. So, what is all this about and why do you think I'll be mad?"

"Well, we got a visit from a very lovely soul named Doris. She has a son, named Dan, who needs to meet someone who will help him learn how to live."

"I don't like the direction this conversation is going." I said.

"We thought you would both work well together. You'll put a little spontaneity in his life and he will put a little stability in your life. You must admit you could use some."

"I'm not exactly pleased with your interference, no matter how well meant. What would you have done if I had told him that I didn't want to marry him? I have to do some thinking about this situation."

"Would it help if I told you that he really does need you?" She asked hesitantly.

"You and the others need to know that I'm not in love with him."

"It doesn't matter, he loves you and I think that's all that is needed for now."

"Well, I've got a lot to think about so make yourself scarce, all of you." I said, feeling the others hovering close by.

It took me a few days to come to terms with the idea of them interfering in my life no matter how well- meant. I decided that I couldn't back out just because I didn't like them interfering in my life. I couldn't exactly tell Dan about my conversation with Hannah and that his mother was in on it. On May 22nd, 1988 we were married, and my son was born in March of 1990.

It's rather ironic that they chose to put two exact opposites together. I think even God had a big laugh on both of us. Who says God doesn't have a sense of humor, he certainly did in our case. So you see, even though you can communicate with the other side, that doesn't mean they are going to tell you everything. Information is given on a need-to-know basis, and you may not need to know. That was 26 years ago and we're still together, so you see divine interference is not all bad.

VEGAS DEMON

One would think that all dark energy comes from negative entities such as demons, minions, and ghosts. But this is not true; 90% of the negative energy in the world is created by man. What does that say about mankind?

You don't have to see the dark ones to know that they are close by. You can feel it; the air suddenly becomes heavy, you may experience nausea, the room suddenly feels freezing cold, you may smell rotting meat or sulfur, and you feel a sense of uneasiness in the pit of your stomach.

I was in Las Vegas, giving a lecture in preparation for the completion of my first book. People were calling and coming to my host's home for healings and readings. I had just stopped to take a lunch break when suddenly I sensed a presence of evil close by. I looked over at my host and asked, "When is my next appointment scheduled?"

She checked her schedule book and said "The next person isn't scheduled until one o'clock so we can have some lunch. Why do you want to know, is there a problem?"

I looked at her and shook my head. "Someone's coming, and they have a demon attached to them."

"How do you know someone's coming?" she asked.

"Because I can feel them coming, right here," I said, holding a fist over my stomach area.

I felt an internal coldness and a sense of foreboding that always warns me when evil is present. She looked at me nervously, and then the doorbell rang.

"Don't worry about the demon it can't get past the line of protection surrounding the house. That's why I had you place a line of blessed salt around the house, so nothing negative could enter prior or during my visit." The doorbell rang again and she looked at me nervously then went to answer it. A young woman stood in the doorway.

"I've been trying to get through to you on the phone for the past two days. I wanted to schedule an appointment for a healing. The line was always busy. No matter what time I called, I could never seem to get through. I decided to take a chance and stop by the house to see if I could schedule a healing." The woman said, looking over at me.

I looked at my host, "Lunch can wait, because I need to take care of this right away." I said, giving her a meaningful look. "Let's go somewhere private so we can talk." I took her into another room.

Shutting the door I asked, "So how long have you had the demon attached to you?"

She looked at me in shock. "Is that what's wrong with me? All my life I've felt like I had a black cloud hanging over my head. I've had nothing but bad luck for as long as I can remember. I lost my parents when I was twelve; my stepbrother has been stealing money from my trust fund and I've always been in a lot of physical pain."

Again I sensed the dark presence; turning my head I could see the demon outside the property and it was furious. I opened myself up to contact the angelic plane.

"God please send me some help in the form of an Archangel to remove the demon."

I heard a soft voice say "Child I will send Ezekiel and Michael to deal with the demon. Tell the woman that the demon had been trying to prevent her from contacting you. It knew that if she did come, its presence would be revealed and it would be banished."

I felt overpowering warmth spread through my body and knew that the Archangels were next to me.

The next moment I felt them leave. Looking out the window I could see Michael was on one side of the demon and Ezekiel on the other side. They seemed to be wrestling with it. The next thing I knew all three of them disappeared. I smiled to myself and said "thank you," out loud. The woman looked at me in inquiry.

"I asked God to send an Archangel to take care of the demon. He sent Michael and Ezekiel. They were here for a moment and then I saw one on each side of the demon and it was struggling to get away. Then all three of them disappeared. You won't have to worry about the demon anymore." I smiled reassuringly at her.

"Are you sure it won't be back?" she asked nervously.

"When God has a demon removed, it never comes back."

"God said to let you know that it was the demon who was trying to prevent you from coming here. Our phone line was not busy all the time; it was the demon trying to prevent itself from being found out. You'll find that your streak of bad luck and that dark cloud hanging over your head will no longer prevent you from living your life.

"I can hardly believe it, I feel so much lighter, as if a great weight has been lifted from me. Thank you, thank you so much for your help in removing it." She said, starting to cry.

"Don't thank me, thank God; He's the one who sent the Archangels to remove the demon. I think your brother is going to find that the shoe's on the other foot. Now it's you who will be set free, free to live your life in the light."

I did a reading for her to let her know that the future was indeed filled with light, and she wouldn't have to worry about the dark-one anymore.

It is possible for a person to have a demon or a negative entity attached to them, and is unaware of it. It does not happen often but when it does your life is pure hell. Most people pass it off as bad luck or they may think they're cursed, when in actuality it is so much worse than what they think.

I AM NOT WHAT I APPEAR TO BE

Around 20 years ago was the first time that I saw an angelic being with my physical eye. Usually I see them with my inner eye. It was around 8:30 at night and I was in my bedroom sitting on the bed preparing to meditate. The room was dark and peaceful.

Closing my eyes I focused on the image of my sister Ann, who is one of my guides.

"Ann, don't you think it's time that you showed yourself to me? I had begun my breathing exercises when I noticed a light that penetrated my eyelids. A first I thought it might have been lights from a car going by so I didn't open my eyes. When the light didn't fade or diminish I decided to open my eyes. Upon opening them I saw a white mist begin to form in the bedroom doorway. I wasn't afraid; rather I was intensely curious as to what it could be. At first it was just a fluctuating white mass which slowly turned into the outline of a woman.

The longer I looked at the form the clearer it became and it looked exactly like the image I see in my head of my sister Ann. "Wow, she's an actual angel." I said not realizing that I spoke aloud.

"Of course I'm an 'actual angel', what else did you expect? You always knew I was an angel."

"Yeah, but it's different from actually seeing you with my eyes."

"Maybe you don't like the wings? I can make them any size or get rid of them completely if I want to." She said fitting the actions to her words. "Do you like the color?" She asked changing the color and then removing them completely. "I call it silver pearl." She twirled around in front of me wearing a dress straight out of the forties. Her hair was swept up in a style of the same era.

"Why have you suddenly decided to show yourself to me in the physical world? It's not like I haven't asked you before, why now?"

"Well you've never really needed to see me before. You've always seemed content to see me as an image in your head. Lately, you've begun to doubt yourself and your gifts. I knew you needed something to reaffirm your belief in yourself and your gifts."

"I thought you guys were not supposed to appear in angelic form. I was under the impression that you needed a very good reason, like life or death situations."

"Most of the time you are correct but there are certain special cases that require it. You do a lot of work for God and according to Him you have always held a special place in His heart."

"Me! What have I ever done that makes me so special? I'm just a regular person with no particular or outstanding attributes. I've never done anything in this life time that I would have thought was special, except maybe serve Him."

"You've done more than you know and you are much more than the sum of this lifetime. But you are not ready, to know the full extent of why this is." She said mysteriously.

"I guess it's a need-to-know basis and I don't need to know."

"What is the significance of the angels' wings? When I see you in my mind's eye, you don't have any."

She roared with laughter. "I thought you might get a kick out of it."

I laughed "Well they certainly were spectacular looking wings. How did you pick that particular color for your wings?

"We can project any image that we want to; it's all a matter of how we want to be perceived. Sometimes we'll look into your mind and choose an image that you have of what we should look like. That's what negative entities will do to elicit fear which helps them grow stronger. I can give you the image of how I looked in any one of my past lives. I chose to appear to you as I was in the life before I became your sister. I thought it would be easier for you to converse with an adult. As you know I was just shy of 2 months old when I died as your sister."

"That makes perfect sense; it really would have been strange to hear your voice coming out of a two month old baby. Okay, so it's kind of like in the movie The Matrix, how I see you is a kind of 'residual self-image'."

Ann smiled, "Yes, you are right. It's very simple to project an image into a person's mind. Do you realize that you're the only one outside of perhaps your dogs who can see me? Even our mother does not see me because she doesn't want to see me. Most people don't want to see anything out of the ordinary and therefore you don't see us. If we don't want to be seen, we won't be seen. Very few mortals have the ability to see us if we don't want them to. A lot of people can sense us, but few people like you can see us even when we don't want to be seen. "

"So why doesn't Hannah show herself to me?" I asked.

Suddenly a voice coming from my right said, "Look over here and you can see if I resemble your image of me."

Turning my head to the right I saw the image of a short thin woman. She was dressed in a three quarter-length cotton dress and her hair pulled back into a bun. She was smiling at me reassuringly.

"I know you died in the 1700's but your clothes are from a later time period." I said looking at her in inquiry.

She chuckled, "Remember it's all about self-image, and I do prefer the mid length dresses to the floor length ones. I always hated how the hem of the dresses would be forever dirty from dragging the ground," She said, rolling her eyes. "Oh, right," I said trying not to laugh, "I'll try to remember."

"This will probably be one of the only times you will see us with your physical eyes." Ann told me.

"Why is that? I asked her

"You needed this validation, because you were beginning to doubt yourself, and besides, we're only allowed to show ourselves on rare occasions," she explained. I have not seen them in the physical world since.

SHADOW PERSON

Most of the time psychics and mediums can see through the projected appearance that ghosts like to present. At first, we may perceive them as they want us to see them, but soon the illusion drops away and they are revealed for what they really are. It can be as frightening for them to see us as it is for us to see them. My most recent encounter with a shadow person was when I went to the coast for a couple of days.

It was the week of Thanksgiving 2011; my husband and I decided to visit my cousin who lived at the Oregon coast in Newport. Her husband was ill and could not come up for Thanksgiving, so we decided to take Thanksgiving to him. We were able to book a room with our timeshare at Schooner Landing in Newport.

The first night we were there my husband and son were downstairs in the living room area and I was upstairs in the master bedroom. Suddenly I felt a chill and started looking around for the cause of it.

"June, get down here!" I heard my husband shout.

Jumping up from the bed I hurried down the stairs. My husband was standing in the living room staring into the dining area.

"What's that?" He asked me in a hushed voice.

Looking in the direction he was staring, at first I saw a childlike figure. What I saw was not in correlation with what I was feeling. The sense of dread and feeling cold to my core was a clear indication of a negative entity.

"Mom, what is that thing? I don't like it, it makes me feel scared and I want to throw up." My son said keeping his eyes on the figure.

"It's not what it appears to be, it's not a child. It's a negative entity I need to look deeper to see its true form." I told him. I decided to expand my protective shield around my husband and son before unmasking it. Concentrating on the entity I began to see what was hidden behind the childish mask. It tried to keep me from seeing its true form. Every time I would get close to seeing what it really was it put up another barrier. At last I managed to see what it really was, a show creature.

Staring at it intently I said, "You need to go back where you came from, now." The minute I voiced the command it turned, looked at me and showed its true form for all to see. In the instant I thought to banish it, it read my thoughts and disappeared out of the condo through the sliding glass door.

Visibly shaken my son asked, "Was that one of those shadow people? That's the same feeling I got when I went into that ceramic shop in Damascus. I could hardly wait to get out of there. I made myself stay and look around to see if I could find it and I could feel it following me."

"You should have had you're protection in place or let me know when you go so I can extend mine around you. The demon that resides there is attached to the land not the buildings."

"Well if that's any indication of what they can, do I don't want to see another one! It gave me the creeps and made me feel sick to my stomach." My husband said.

I looked at him with a slight smile and said, "Welcome to my world."

I headed back upstairs to the bedroom where I found my sister sitting on the bed. "That creature certainly chose the wrong place to be didn't it? No telling what kind of mischief it would have gotten up if I hadn't influenced Dan into going into the kitchen for a snack."

"I was wondering why he noticed it; it's so unlike him to notice anything paranormal."

"Well I figured it wouldn't hurt him to get a little taste of what you have to deal with. Maybe he would be a little more understanding of what you have to go through. As for Ray, he needs to be aware of what those creatures look like, so that he will know to steer clear of them in the future."

"What's up with that shadow person? Isn't it unusual for a shadow person to take on the façade of a human? They usually don't try to hide what they are, that's more of a demonic trick. I've never heard of them showing themselves as anything other than what they are. Why do they use the pretense?"

"It couldn't sense your presence at first and was caught off guard when it saw you. It tried to hide by taking on the form of a child. But once it could sense the presence of a light being, meaning Michael, it tried to hide from him by showing itself as a ghost instead of what it really is. Those things will never learn that we're far too clever to be fooled by them, stupid creatures." She said shaking her head.

"Remember what your grandma told you, 'just when you think you have the other side all figured out, you don't'. Never think that you know everything there is to know about the paranormal. I can tell you right now, even with all your knowledge and experience, you haven't seen everything the dark ones can do. For that matter you haven't seen everything that we can do either."

"I understand that you can't think like a human in dealing with the other side. You're not bound by laws of psychics like we are here on this plane of existence. What can a person do if you can't protect yourself against a physical assault?"

"You're still thinking like a human, you have to think like them. If they can shove or scratch you using the energy they project, you can do the same. You have to believe and learn to use the energy that is a part of you. All living things have energy fields and different vibrations; you just have to learn how to manipulate the energy around you as well as your own energy. If you're strong enough you can use their energy against them."

"And are you guys going to teach me how to do it? Because, if not, it might take me a while to figure out how I can use their energy against them."

"Yes, we'll teach you how to do it. It's not something you can learn overnight it takes practice. It is well worth learning; very few humans have the knowledge, and ability to do it."

From that day forward I started keeping a protective barrier around myself.

CAN YOU HELP ME?

Usually when a person sees a ghost, they automatically assume they're evil. That is not always the case. They may be lost, confused, disoriented or just not know that they are dead. It sometimes happens with those souls who have a traumatic, or sudden death.

My cousin José was just such a ghost; his death was both sudden and traumatic. José was working in a logging camp with a friend of his in eastern Oregon. They finished work one day and decided to go down to the local bar and have a few drinks. They were both under age and were not supposed to be served alcohol. By the time they were ready to leave they were both drunk. José crawled into the back of his Ford van, and went to sleep. His buddy drove while my cousin slept. The young man took a curve too fast and hit a telephone pole. He was thrown clear but the pole landed on José breaking several bones and putting him in a coma.

José and I grew up together in the home of our grandparents for the first 5 years of our lives. We were close growing up and spent a lot of time together. I was visiting his house the day he told his mother he was going to change schools.

"Mom, I've decided to go to public high school." José told her.

"What, are you out of your mind? No way, you're going to go to a private high school. I found an all-boy's school in Portland. You can take a bus there and home."

"There's a perfectly good high school 2 miles from here, and that's where I want to go."

"You are not going to public high school; they are riddled with drugs and violence. I've made my decision and that's the end of the discussion." She said, turning to leave the room.

"I am not going; I already signed up for high school."

She turned to look at him and I could see how angry she was. "If you go to the public high school, then I don't want anything more to do with you!" She said angrily, walking away.

He turned and looked at me and I shrugged my shoulders. "She means it you know. She's a lot like mom, very controlling. What are you going to do?"

"She'll come around; I'm going to the regular high school."

I didn't tell him that I had a bad feeling about his decision. I knew that the state his mind was in, that he would think I was siding with his mother.

After José started public school; he got mixed up with a bad crowd and got heavily into drugs. He dropped out of school during his third year. He was still living at home when my grandmother had a diabetic reaction and needed to be taken to the hospital. She called my mother's house and I came to take her to the hospital. José came out of the back door while I was getting her into the car.

"Where are you taking her?" He asked.

I looked up startled; I didn't know that he was staying at her home. Looking into his face I noticed that his normally brown eyes were black and devoid of any emotion. In fact it was like there was darkness in his soul. I had never seen anything like it before. He must have noticed my reaction to him because he smiled at me. It was not a pleasant smile, but one full of pure evil.

"You don't care about anyone anymore. There's nothing left in you that is good, I don't know you anymore. You need to leave and not come back, you don't belong here anymore." I told him angrily. I could sense the demon that was influencing him.

He ultimately left shortly after that and I never saw him alive again. Right after he left home I left for the military. Whenever I tried to connect with him psychically I could feel the demon trying to block the connection.

I got a call from my mother in November of the following year to let me know José was dead. I came home on leave for the funeral and he was buried on my birthday.

I found out later that it took the hospital 3 days after the accident to find his mother. He had no emergency contact listed on his employment form. He died before she could be contacted and she never saw him alive again. He never got the chance to ask for her forgiveness before he died. Twenty-eight years later he came to me.

It was the beginning of summer, and I was sitting out on my deck watching the sun go down. The air suddenly turned cold, but it was 80 degrees outside.

"Who's there? I asked telepathically.

The response I received surprised me. "It's me, José. I need your help."

"Why after all these years do you suddenly come to me wanting help?"

"I have spent the last 27 of your years in limbo, unable to ask for help or communicate with anyone in the physical plane. I was put there for the pain I caused so many people during my last lifetime."

"Okay, so what do you want? You've obviously done your time for your transgressions on the other side. Did you ever shake loose the demonic influence before you crossed?"

"Yes, but I can't rest until my mother forgives me for all the pain I caused her."

"Wow, you don't want much do you? That's a tall order and I can't see her doing me any favors. Why haven't you reached out to me before this?"

"She is going to cross soon and she needs to forgive me while she's still in this lifetime." José said.

"Let me think about this, I have to do it in such a way that she doesn't know it's coming from me." I knew that it wouldn't do any good for me to ask my aunt to forgive him. "I'll get back to you when I figure out a plan."

"Thanks, I'm sorry for any pain I caused you when I was alive, please forgive me."

"I forgive you now that you've learned your lesson. Now beat it while I come up with a plan."

The following week I called my cousin José's sister, Judy; his mother lived with her.

"Hey, I've got a bit of a problem and I need your help.

"Okay, what's up?"

"José stopped by the other day."

"You mean my brother Jose?" she asked in surprise.

"Yes, your brother José. He wanted me to ask your mom to forgive him for the hurt he caused her when he was alive."

"Wow, what a trip! What did you say?"

"Well I know your mom won't listen to either of us, so I thought maybe we could get Nellie to talk to her about it. She thinks the sun rises and sets around her great-granddaughter."

"Great idea, I'll talk to her tonight about it. Did he say why he waited so long to come through?"

"Yes, he said he had to spend 27 years in limbo thinking about the pain he caused in his lifetime. When we cross over we examine our lives from the perspective of the people around us. It is an enlightening experience."

"I guess he would have a lot to make up for in his later years, considering all the drugs he did." I agreed with her but did not tell her about the negative attachment he had the last time I saw him.

A few weeks went by with no word from my cousin, then, one afternoon I received a call from her. "Well, it took Nellie a couple of times asking, but mom finally, grudgingly agreed to forgive José."

"Great now maybe he can get some peace."

"I hope so; I can't imagine what it would be like reliving all the hurtful things you did over and over again."

"Well we did our part to help him; I'll let you know if I hear from him."

"Thanks, of course, I won't tell mom!" she said laughing.

A few days later I was busy writing in my office when I heard José.

"You did it; you got her to forgive me."

"Well it was actually Nellie, not me."

"But if you hadn't found a way to do it, then I wouldn't have been released from my self-inflicted purgatory. I can finally be at peace. You won't hear from me again until I am reborn into the family. I won't ever make the same mistakes I made in this lifetime, I promise." And he left.

It was not until 2009, when that same great-granddaughter, Nellie, who helped her great grandmother to forgive her son, José, had a son of her own; that I knew he had returned.

THE LAST HURRAH

Sometimes the soul can appear to a person just at the moment of death before they cross over completely. Everyone has heard stories of a person showing themselves to a loved one right after they died. Once in a while you will get a soul who lets you know they have died by moving an object, showing themselves, or even a familiar scent of perfume or the aroma of pipe tobacco. I have been nursing for over 30 years and have experienced this several times in not only my personal, but professional life.

The first time this happened I was nine years old. I was at my grandparents' house, and while I was there, my grandfather died. He had a heart condition for several years. He went into the bathroom to take a bath to get ready for my older brother's birthday party. I was sitting at the dining room table talking with my grandmother. The house was designed in such a way that you had to walk through my grandfather's small bedroom to reach the bathroom. With his door open you could see the entrance to the bathroom. Suddenly my grandmother looked up and said, "Ray?"

She got up from her chair and went to the bathroom door, knocking on it, "Ray, are you okay? Ray?" When he did not answer, she opened the door and found him dead in the bathtub. She came out of the bathroom and walked into the living room and sat down. Her face was as white as the tablecloth on the table where I sat. She sat very still for a few moments then reached for the phone next to her. I watched as she called for an ambulance. She got up, came over and sat down next to me at the table to wait.

"Turning to look at her I asked, "Grandma, why did grandpa leave?"

She looked at me in a kind of dazed manner and seemed unsurprised that I knew he was gone, even though she did not tell me.

"It was his time, I think that the water was too cold and too much of a shock for his heart to withstand." She said, gently.

I accepted the news without question and waited with my grandmother for the ambulance.

The ambulance people came and took his body away. Immediately after, my cousin arrived with her husband, Bob. No one in the family really liked Bob, especially my grandfather. He always felt something wasn't quite right about him and he couldn't stand to have him around. To keep peace in the family, he never said anything to anyone but we all knew it. Grandma told them about grandpa and my cousin began to cry. Like me, she lived with our grandparents for most of her early life.

I couldn't understand why she was crying. I knew that grandpa was still in the house somewhere. I could feel his comfort and warmth near me. I was too young to understand that she could not see him like I could.

I was sitting at the dining room table; I had a clear view of my grandfather's bedroom and the bathroom door. Bob got up and went into the bathroom. It couldn't have been more than a minute or two after the door was closed, when I saw the big old heavy wooden dresser of my grandfather's suddenly tip over blocking the bathroom door. It seemed to happen in slow motion. I didn't say a thing, just waited to see what would happen next. Grandpa appeared beside the dresser, gave me a smile and disappeared. I was the only one who knew my grandpa tipped the dresser over.

A few minutes later I heard Bob wiggling the handle of the bathroom door. I think at first he thought that the door was just stuck. Then I could hear him trying to push the door open, but it wouldn't budge. The next thing I knew he was shouting for help.

"Hey, somebody let me out of here, the doors stuck." he yelled pounding on the door.

It took three people to right the dresser so Bob could get out of the bathroom. Boy was he mad.

"Ha, Ha, very funny, who is the wise guy who tipped over the dresser?" He asked angrily.

"We don't know how it got there." His wife said. "It took 3 of us to get the thing back upright."

"Grandpa did it. He never really liked you, you know." I said boldly, as children often do.

The room became silent for a moment or two.

"Shut up you little brat." Bob said angrily, glaring at me.

I wasn't afraid because I knew grandpa was still there and he wouldn't let anything happen to me. I didn't say anything more, but I looked toward my grandmother who gave me a knowing look. Later, when everything was quiet, I told my grandmother what I saw.

"Grandpa really did push the dresser over, just to scare Bob a little." I said.

She smiled at me. "This is our little secret, just between you and me."

I never did tell anyone about it, but who would believe a nine year old?

LETTING GO

When I was 11 years old, I had my first sleepover at a friend's house. I woke suddenly in the early morning, around 3 am. I heard the stairs creaking and went to investigate. When I arrived at the top of the stairs I stopped in surprise. The wooden rocking chair that usually sat at the foot of the stairs was now walking up the stairs by its self. It was as if someone were lifting it and sitting it down, one step at a time. Suddenly, I heard the voice of my friend's dad, Gene, coming from the bottom of the stairs. I thought at first he was talking to me, but I soon realized that he was speaking to whatever force was moving the chair.

"I've told you before to stop making noise in the middle of the night. Now bring that chair back downstairs."

The chair stopped where it was precariously perched on the stair below me. Suddenly the chair wobbled. It was as if whatever was holding it suddenly released its grip. As it started to fall Gene made a mad dash up the stairs to grab it. As he caught the chair he saw me standing at the top. "It's alright you can come down, she won't hurt you, there's no need to be afraid."

Gene placed the chair back where it belonged near the bottom of the stairs and motioned for me to come downstairs. I hesitantly complied and followed him into the sitting room next to where the chair sat, giving it a wide birth.

"You see that chair," he said pointing to the rocking chair, "it belonged to an old woman who used to own this house. From what I've learned, she lived here for over sixty years and died here in the house. She is not a bad ghost; she just wants to stay here in her beloved home. I've known for a long time that she was here, but I let her stay hoping she would cross over on her own. Since it doesn't look like it's going to happen anytime soon I think we need to help her, don't you?" He asked, sitting down.

I nodded in agreement, drawing closer to his side, still wary of the chair.

"What if she doesn't want to go?" I asked him

"I can't make them go, it's their choice, but I can be pretty persuasive." He said smiling at me. "This is not the first time I have helped someone cross over. Sometimes you just need to sit down and talk to them. Sometimes they don't know they are dead. This is what you need to explain to them. Let them know that they have loved ones waiting for them on the other side."

Turning he looked at the rocking chair which had begun to rock. "Abby it's time for you to move on. I've waited patiently for you to cross on your own. I know you want to be with your family and I promise I will do what I can to help your son to move on."

As I stared at the chair I could see a form start to take shape. I could see it was a very small, fragile looking, old woman with short, curly gray hair. She smiled and winked at me. I knew she was aware that I could see her.

She looked at me and asked for my help. "Will you tell him I understand and appreciate what he's trying to do for me? He's right, it is time I joined the others, and my son will come in his own time." She sighed heavily.

Turning to Gene I relayed the woman's message, "The lady wants me to tell you she understands that you are trying to help her. She says you are right, it is time for her to join her family."

He looked at me in surprise for a moment, and then smiled. "Well you tell her I'm glad she's ready to cross over."

"She can hear you, I don't need to tell her, just talk to her. I'll tell you what she says," I told him earnestly.

"All you have to do is look for the light; it will be the brightest light you've ever seen, full of love and warmth. Can you see the light?" He asked.

"I can't see it, wait a minute, there it is. Would you look at that? There's my husband and my daughter!" She said tears of joy running down her face.

"She sees the light and her family, she's so happy."

"Good, now all you have to do is walk into the light, and you'll be with your family."

Looking at me she said, "Tell him 'thank you' for putting up with me all these years, and for helping my son."

As we watched, the chair suddenly rocked wildly and then stopped completely. I turned to look at Gene and said," She's gone, you won't see her again. She said to tell you thank you for putting up with her all these years and for helping her son."

Looking at me he said, "You're a strange little thing. You surprised me tonight, but then I should have known; you have the eyes of an old soul."

I ignored his comment. I asked curiously, "Who is the man in the garage, is that her son?"

"Yes, I don't want you going out there by yourself. He's not a nice ghost and I don't know if he would try to hurt you," he said to me. "My wife is afraid to go into the garage because there have been times when a hangman's noose was found hanging over the rafters. I think he may have hung himself. I don't know for sure, but everything points to that. If he did, that means he may not be a good ghost."

"He's not bad, just afraid."

He looked at me seriously and asked, "What makes you say that?"

"He said he wasn't feeling good for a long time, he hurt so much he couldn't take the pain. He says that he just wanted someone to know he's there and maybe help him."

"Well I'll work on helping him. Maybe he's afraid to cross over because he killed himself. Some people believe if you kill yourself you can't go to heaven."

We talked for a little while longer, me asking questions and him explaining as best he could.

"I want you to remember something very important, June Ann." He said, "Don't ever try to cross over a soul on your own. You're too young to know what you're getting into and I don't want you to get a spirit attachment."

I looked at him, "What's a spirit attachment?"

"It can happen when you try to help a soul cross over and they don't want to go, or they're bad. Once they become attached to you they are hard to get rid of, and some can make your life a living hell." He said.

Curious, I asked, "What do they do?"

"They can make you have terrible nightmares, they can make people hate you and cause arguments that break up families and in some cases they can hurt you and even possess your body."

"I wouldn't like that; I guess I'll wait until I'm older to help the ones who ask me for help. My grandma can help me learn how to help them; she does it all the time."

"She can hear the ghosts?"

"Yes, she says all the women in our family have helped them for generations."

"Yes, I think you should ask your grandma to help you, it sounds like she knows what she is doing." Smiling at me, he stood up "Well its back to bed for you."

"Okay." I went back to bed and fell fast asleep. I never did find out what happened with the woman's son because shortly after that Gene's wife was diagnosed with terminal cancer.

A VISIT TO THE THEATER

A few years ago I was visiting my friend Grace in LaGrande, Oregon. It's a 6 hour drive from my house and I got there in the early evening. The following morning we decided to go into town for breakfast. As I was drinking my coffee Grace brought up the subject of a local haunting. "Hey, I wanted to talk to you about a friend of mine. Her name is Sheri and she owns one of the old theaters in LaGrande."

"Yes, what do you want to talk about?" I asked, trying to figure out where she was going with this.

"Well, she's been telling me she thinks the theater is haunted. I told her you were coming to visit this weekend. She was wondering if you could drop by the theater and let her know what you think. I told her I would ask you, and let her know. I wasn't sure how long you were staying, so I didn't know if you would have the time to do it."

"Well, when did she want to do this?"

"It will have to be during the day, most likely in the morning because the theater is open from noon until midnight."

"Well," I asked, "do you think she'd be willing to do it tomorrow morning?"

"Let me give her a call and find out if that's okay with her." She had to leave a message for Sheri on her voicemail to get back to us.

We finished our breakfast and were just about to leave when her phone rang. It was Sheri on the other end; we made arrangements to meet the next morning at 10 am, in front of the old theater. Grace and I spent the rest of the day catching up on the latest news and having a leisurely dinner. The next morning I followed Grace to the theater in my car. I planned to leave after my walk-through of the theater. I wasn't sure how long it would take, but I knew it would take me six hours to get home, and I wanted to leave before dark.

The moment I parked in front of the theater, I felt the presence of multiple spirits. A woman was standing by the front door with keys in her hand. Getting out of the car I noticed that Grace was already talking to the woman. I locked my car and headed towards them. Grace introduced us, and Sheri thanked me for taking the time to come and do the walk-through.

"I want to thank you for doing this for me. I know you're here visiting Grace and I appreciate anything that you can do to help me."

"It's no problem. I do this sort of thing periodically. Let's go inside shall we?"

Sheri unlocked the door and motioned for me to go inside.

Stepping through the antique door I opened myself completely. "Do you know you have four ghosts in the building?" I asked her.

"I kind of thought that I might have one, but not four of them." she said surprised.

"Well, there are four distinct entities; three in residence and one that comes in visitation."

"That explains all of the strange things happening since I bought the theater 10 years ago."

"Don't give me any information because I like to see what I can pick up on," I said, clearing my mind. I started to walk around the theater and get a feel for what was going on and what people might experience in relation to the ghosts.

"Sheri, where's the projection room? I'm being drawn towards the projection room."

"It's this way." She said, heading towards a closed-door on the left side of the lobby. As she unlocked the door I saw a set of stairs.

As I reach the top of the stairs I entered a small room with projection equipment. There was modern equipment as well as vintage equipment. Placing my hand on the vintage projector I saw the image of a man who felt very much present. Turning, I headed back down the stairs to rejoin Grace and Sheri.

"If you both just want to wait here I'll make my way around the theater and then meet you back here."

"Alright, we'll actually wait for you in the employee break room through that door." She said pointing to the door marked private on the right side of the lobby.

"Okay I'll meet you there when I'm finished; it shouldn't take too long depending upon what I find." Turning, I headed towards the theater. Standing for a moment just inside the seating area I could feel the presence of a child and a woman. I could feel the child following me as I made my way down towards the old stage area. As I reached the stage area I noticed a door off to the left side of the stage.

As I headed towards the door the child spirit hung back as if reluctant to go any closer to the door. As I touch the handle I could feel that something negative waited on the other side. Taking a deep breath I reinforced my white light energy field surrounding my body. Opening the door I stepped into what must have been a large dressing room. I could feel the presence of something negative and menacing. Walking over to the far end of the room I felt a shift in time. With my inner eye I could see the land that this building sat on before the building was here. This told me the negative presence I was sensing was attached to the land and not the building. Leaving the room and closing the door, I headed back towards the lobby. The child was following behind me again.

Joining Sheri and Grace in the break room, I sat down for a moment to gather my thoughts. "Well, that was interesting. You have four separate entities from three different times." "What do you mean from different times? It never occurred to me that ghosts could be from different times. How is that possible? Do they interact with each other?" She asked in amazement.

"Ghosts can be from different times and interact with each other, or they may choose not to interact. Time has no meaning to them. If they don't know they're dead, they won't always notice the passage of time. If they are aware of their own death, they will see the changes."

"Wow, that's weird," she said.

"The first spirit is a woman in a white Victorian dress, named Sarah. She is grounded here, which means she is either unable to leave or doesn't want to. The second is a young boy of the same era. He appears to be around eight and he comes in visitation. That means he moves from the physical world through the veil to the angelic realm."

"Why does he come here?" she wanted to know. I paused a minute asking the boy telepathically his name and why he visits here.

"Hi, I'm Sam; I'm here to visit my mom. I've been trying to get her to come with me to the other side, but she won't. She says she's afraid that God will find her guilty of something, but she won't tell me what. Can you help get her to come with me?"

"How did you die?"

"My mom got real sick and she died, then I got sick."

Turning back to Sheri I relayed to her what he had said. "He is the woman's son, Sam, who died of the same disease that had taken his mother's life- smallpox. He comes in visitation to try to get her to come back with him into the light, but she always refuses. He doesn't know why she won't go but he wants me to try to help her cross over into the light. I'll have to talk to her to find out what's going on."

Tuning out the living, I focused on connecting with Sarah. Establishing the connection, I asked, "Sarah why don't you want to cross into the light?"

"Because I abandoned my son!" she replied sobbing.

"What makes you think you abandoned your son?"

"I died; I should have fought harder to stay alive! I tried, honestly I did, but before I knew it I was dead. At first I couldn't seem to find my son. Then when I did find him, all I could do is watch helplessly as he grew sick, and died."

"Sarah, it's not your fault, you both died, thousands of people died from smallpox."

"They did? I didn't know so many people died. I'm afraid that God will think that I abandoned my son if I go into the light. I'm worried that I won't be able to be with him. Here at least I can see him when he comes to visit me."

"Sarah, God knows you didn't abandon your son. He knows how much you love him. You died from an illness that you couldn't recover from, so did your son."

"Yeah mom, God told me that He doesn't blame you for anything. Can we go now?" Sam said pulling on his mother's hand.

She turned to look at me and I gave her a reassuring smile. "Go ahead, do you see the light?"

She nodded, "It's so beautiful and I can feel His love coming from the light." She turned and smiled at me before walking hand in hand with her son into the light.

"Are they gone?" Sheri asked. "I feel like they've gone."

"Yes she and her son have gone for good."

A third ghost came into the room and looked at me. He was tall, lanky and looked to be in his sixties. His suit was old, neatly pressed and looked like old pictures I had seen from the 1940s era.

"Hello, who are you?"

"My name is Bradley; I used to work here when the theater first opened. I was in charge of the stage, and the projection room." He said proudly.

"Why haven't you crossed over?"

"It's like this; I loved every moment that I spent in this old theater. I would work all day and my wife would bring me lunch and stay for the show. We never had a family, and after sickness took my wife, I spent most of my time here. When I had a heart attack, and died here, I just couldn't bear to leave," he explained.

"What about your wife, don't you miss her?"

"I do but she comes and sees me when she can, she has an important job that she's doing for God. So I know we wouldn't see much of each other on the other side," he said shrugging.

"So what do you do here at the theater?"

"I keep an eye on the kids who work here to make sure they're doing their job. I know Sheri is busy so I try to help her out. There are a couple of kids who don't always do their jobs. They would rather be on their phones or messing around. I try to get them to behave by showing myself to them." He chuckled. "It scares the pants off of them."

Laughing, I turned to Sheri, and told her what Bradley had said about the kids working there. "I know the kids he's talking about." She said. "I've long suspected they were fooling around on the job."

"Can you ask her if I can stay? I promise to keep my eye on the kids and make sure they're doing what they're supposed to. I promise not to scare them too often, only if they are messing around."

Turning to Sheri I relayed his request, "He wants to know if you will allow him to stay. He promises to behave himself, and watch over the theater."

"Okay. Bradley, you can stay." She agreed.

Bradley disappeared, and I felt the fourth spirit enter the room. This spirit had a whole different feel about it. It felt dark, oppressive and sinister. It was definitely a negative entity, and not one of my favorite kinds to deal with.

"Why is it so cold all of a sudden?" Sheri wanted to know.

I was already aware of the temperature drop in the room. "The other three ghosts were not negative, but this one definitely is. This one was nasty in life, and he is nasty in death."

There was a noticeable change in the atmosphere; the air seemed heavier and darker.

"Get out witch, you are not wanted here. Leave while you still can." It said, laughing, darkly.

"I'm not a witch, and I'm not leaving. We have business together, you and I. If anyone is going to leave, it's going to be you." I responded with a smile.

"I'm not leaving, and you can't make me, witch!" he growled, darkly.

"What's wrong? What's happening?" Sheri and Grace wanted to know.

"Why are you here and what do you want?"

"I like it here; there is plenty of negative energy to feed off of."

"Well now, let's see who and what you are." Looking past the image it was projecting in my mind, I dug deeper to see its real face. Suddenly I could see moving images like flipping the pages of a picture book very fast. I could see a man shooting and killing Native American women and children in a village. Then the scene changed and it was white settlers that were being killed. The final scene showed the same man torturing and strangling several women. As the last scene faded, I realized this man had enjoyed killing and torturing people.

"Stay out of my head witch!" He shouted in my head.

"Didn't know I could get into your head the way you can get into mine, did you? Well, you're going to leave whether you like it or not, and I don't have to do a thing but utter one word," I said smiling.

It laughed, sending a shiver up my spine, as I'm sure it was intended to. "And what is that one word." He wanted to know.

"Michael." As the name entered my mind, the Archangel Michael appeared behind him.

"No!" He screamed as Michael wrapped his arms around him, and they both disappeared.

"What happened? It's not cold anymore?" Sheri asked.

In the next instant Michael, the Archangel appeared beside me, and gave me a wink. "He's locked in limbo now, so you don't have to worry about him bothering anyone."

"It is gone. God sent Michael, the Archangel, to take him away." I told Grace and Sheri.

"Wonderful, now we don't have to worry about the negative one. Things should be quieter around here now." Sheri sighed in relief. I told Sheri that we should go ahead with her reading and healing, now that I was through dealing with the negative entity.

I finished Sheri's healing and headed back home. After I left, I found out later from Grace that after that night there were no more problems with the negative entity. Bradley still watches over the theater and occasionally appears to the staff.

THE HITCH HIKER

If you think that the only places you find ghosts, or spirits hanging out, is in cemeteries, battlefields or hospitals, you are mistaken. Angels, like ghosts, are everywhere, they are all around us. Sometimes ghosts may be standing by the side of the road waving at you, sitting next to you in a restaurant, or standing next to you at work. Just because you can't feel them, or see them, doesn't mean they are not there.

The ghost of a young girl named Jenny is one I encountered quite frequently. I moved 26 years ago to a farm in rural Oregon. I first noticed Jenny after my husband and I moved into our new house. She was standing by the side of the road waving to me. She had red hair, braids, and was dressed in a long cotton dress and pinafore with a bonnet dangling down her back. I guessed that she must've come across during the wagon train era. It made sense since I live on the Oregon Trail. One day in late fall she decided to pop into the car beside me.

I was headed out by myself to do some shopping when I heard a voice ask, "Where are you going?" It startled me so much I jerked the wheel.

"Don't do that, you nearly caused me to have an accident." I scolded her.

"I'm sorry; I didn't mean to scare you, I thought you would feel me pop in."

"Normally I would, but I have a lot on my mind this morning. Why are you still hanging around here? Why haven't you crossed over? Don't you want to be with your family?"

"Yes and no," she said cryptically

"What does that mean?"

"It's like this, my momma died when I was little and my father remarried. The woman he married had children of her own and didn't really want me around. She always made me do all the chores by myself, while her children didn't have to do anything. I tried to tell my papa, but he wouldn't listen."

"I can see why you wouldn't want to be with them, but what about your momma? I'm sure she's waiting for you."

"She comes to visit me sometimes, but I have fun watching things change. I try to look for people to talk to like you. It's hard to find anyone to talk to but other spirits and they are no fun."

"Why don't you go with your mother when she leaves? You can always come back for a visit you know?"

"You mean I don't have to stay there once I get there?" She seemed genuinely surprised at this bit of information. "No one has ever told me that. I thought once I went over I couldn't come back."

"No, you can always come back and visit whenever you like. Do you know how long it has been since you died?" I asked, and she shook her head. "It has been over 150 years; what do you think of that?"

"Wow, I didn't realize it's been so long. Maybe you are right, maybe I need to cross. When momma comes to visit again, I'll go with her," she promised.

After that first conversation, I saw her quite often in different areas along the road, in about a 4 mile radius. Then I didn't see her again for over a year, until one morning when I was headed to work. She popped into the seat beside me.

"So, how was the crossing?" I asked.

"It was great; I'm with momma most of the time. I was given a small job to do, but when I have some free time I come back and visit. It's just like you said, I can come back and visit." She said, smiling widely.

"Great, I'm glad you are able to visit from time to time."

"I'll only be able to visit for a little longer. I've decided that I want to be in the physical world again. Momma says that she's coming back, too. Won't that be nice, we can be together again just like we used to be?"

"That's wonderful; I hope you have a good time when you come back. I guess I won't be seeing much of you anymore."

"No, but you will find others who need your help."

I saw her again, once or twice over the next five years. I have not seen her since.

HARBOR HAUNTING

Ghost haunts are not restricted to land; they can, and do haunt at sea.

Eight years ago, about a week before December 7th, Pearl Harbor day, and my husband came to me about a dream he had.

"I've had the exact same dream for the last three nights in a row. The dream is so vivid and real that I think someone is trying to tell me something." This was a huge admission, because he did not believe in the paranormal.

"So, tell me what happens in the dream."

"The dream always starts the same. I'm on board the Arizona in Pearl Harbor. I'm below deck in the recreation room."

"How many men were there?" I asked.

"I don't know maybe 20, but I got the impression there were others in different parts of the ship."

"What was your position on the ship?"

"I held the ship's Gunner position."

"What is everyone doing, are they talking?"

"There are a bunch of men playing cards. They are talking among themselves. I'm walking through water, like you walk through air. I feel like I'm there, but not really present, kind of how I imagine a ghost would feel. No one is talking to me, or acknowledging me."

"So you are more of an observer?"

"Yeah, something like that, only I can actually feel the water around me."

"What are the men talking about?" I asked.

"It seemed important that I find out what was going on, so I stood quietly, listening intently to their conversation. "They seem to know they are dead, but there is also some confusion, and anger. They know the boat sank, and understand they were trapped below decks. The big topic of conversation was why they were forgotten. They wanted to know why no one came for their bodies. Why they were left entombed within the ship. They are still waiting for someone to come for their bodies. They cannot let go of their deaths because of this, and are unable to cross over completely." He looked at me sadly and asked, "Is there anything you can do to get them out of there? To give them some peace so they can be with their families?"

"I promise I'll do whatever I can to help them, but if they refuse to leave there is nothing I can do about it. It is their choice. Is that all of the dream?"

"No, after the rec room, I'm standing in front of the memorial. I find myself running my finger down the list of men who died. Once I find my name, I wake up and can't remember it. I think if I saw my name again I would know it. Is there any way you can get me a list of the Arizona casualties?"

"Yes, I'll go online and print one out for you."

I found the list of men who were killed on the Arizona, and printed it out for him. He went over the list, and brought it to me when he found his name.

"This is it," he said, "this is who I was." I looked at the name and smiled. The name read Raymond Arthur Roby. We had named our son Ray Arthur after my grandfather. I finally understood why he was happy to give our son that name.

My husband finally had the reason for his unsubstantiated fear of drowning he has had all his life. Pearl Harbor happened in 1941, my husband was born in 1945. His death was so traumatic, and his rebirth so quick, that all of the fear from that past life death came forward with him into his new life.

Later that night during my meditation, I went to the Arizona to talk to the men. Finding myself in the rec room, I saw several spirits gathered, playing various games and talking. A moment or two after I arrived, the first soul noticed me. Getting up from his seat at the table he came over to where I stood in the doorway.

"Have you come for us, we have been waiting so long? Why did they leave us behind?"

"I'm so sorry you were left behind. The ship sank so fast there was no way to get your bodies out."

"So why are you here then, are you dead too?"

As he asked the question I noticed that the others had gathered around us.

"One of you reached out to my husband, and contacted him in a dream."

"That was me; I've been trying to get through to him for some time." A middle aged man toward the back of the men said, holding up his hand. "You are married to Ray, aren't you? He was a very close friend of mine."

"Yes, I am, you finally got through to him. Do you know how long it's been since you died?"

"I know it's been a while, I'm not sure but it can't be too long." He said looking puzzled.

"It's been almost seventy years."

"No, it can't have been that long, Pearl Harbor was just bombed!" the first young man exclaimed in surprise.

"I'm sorry but it's true. Most of the people you have known are either dead, or old. Certainly your parents have crossed over by now."

"What are we going to do? How are we going to get home?"

The older man spoke up again, "That is why I have been trying to get a hold of Ray," he said to the others. "She can help us get home; she is a medium, a person who talks to the dead."

One of the other souls spoke up, "Well I am looking forward to going home. What do we need to do?"

"I any of you wants to go home, close your eyes. Look for a bright, white light in your mind's eye. When you have the image in your mind, open your eyes and start walking towards it. The light will get bigger and brighter as you move towards it. Your family will meet you on the other side."

One by one the souls disappeared into the light, until only one remained.

"Why aren't you crossing over?" I asked.

"I'm not ready yet," was all he said.

The Archangel Michael suddenly appeared beside me.

"You cannot make the soul leave. It is up to the soul if he chooses to come home to the light. He has chosen to remain behind, and I will honor that decision." Michael said. He did not ask the soul why he wanted to stay, but merely respected his wishes. "I will return from time to time to check on the soul to see if he is ready to cross." He promised.

I left knowing that the last soul would be checked on by Michael, and when he was ready to cross, Michael would be there for him.

I let my husband know what had happened, and I could see he was relieved that the souls had crossed.

THE HAUNTED CAR

In 1978, I was serving in the Air Force, and was stationed in Spokane, Washington. I needed reliable transportation so that I could live off base and go home whenever I wanted. I decided to talk to my godfather Smitty about it.

Picking up the phone I called him; "Hey, Smitty I wondered if you would know of anyone who had an inexpensive car for sale?"

"Well it just so happens that you are in luck. I just brought Ruthie a new Honda, so we have an extra car."

"Great, what kind of car is it, and how much do you want for it?"

"It's a 1974 ford Pinto station wagon; I'll sell it to you for five hundred dollars. Will that work for you?"

"Perfect and just the right price too! Is it an automatic or a stick shift? If the car is a stick shift, you will have to teach me how to drive it."

"It's a stick, and it gets great gas mileage. I'll teach you to drive it in no time, after all, I taught Ruthie." He laughed. "Why don't you come down on your next free weekend and pick up the car and you'll have the whole weekend to practice."

"Okay, I'm off in a couple of weeks so I'll be down then."

I knew the car was well-cared for as my godmother had a heart condition, and my godfather always made sure her vehicles were in good shape.

Two weeks later I arrived at my godparent's home to pick up the car. Sliding behind the wheel of the car I experienced a strange sense of uneasiness. I shrugged it off and focused on what Smitty was saying.

"You need to synchronize your gas and clutch, so that you release one and engage the other." Over the next couple of hours I learned how and when to use the clutch. I spent the remainder of the weekend with them and on Sunday afternoon headed back to Spokane.

At first, it was just a vague feeling of unease every time I got behind the wheel. After a month of driving the car, I began to experience visions. Every time I sat in the driver seat, I seemed to be seeing an accident through the eyes of someone else. In the vision I am driving on a long, straight stretch of road. I can see a car coming toward me, then, it suddenly begins to swerve erratically, as if the person driving has lost control. Then the car is headed straight at me, I swerve, trying to miss the oncoming car. The impact seems inevitable, and the vision ends. This vision played out exactly the same each time, like a film caught in a loop. That is when I knew that I was dealing with residual energy that was attached to the car.

I called my godmother to see if she had any information. "What can you tell me about the previous owner of the car?"

"I don't have much information about her, why?" she asked.

"Well, the moment I got in the car I had a kind of uneasy feeling, but I shrugged it off."

"You know, I always thought there was something off about the car, but I just ignored it."

"Every time I get into the car, I see a vision through the eyes of another person. Another car is heading toward me on the wrong side of the road. I never see the actual impact; it ends with the other vehicle coming straight toward me."

"I'm sorry I couldn't be of more help, but that's all I know."

"Well not to worry, I'll figure it out, maybe I'll call my grandmother and see what she says."

"Yeah, she might be able to help you figure it out." She said, and hung up.

I called my grandmother the next day and explained what was happening. "It sounds to me like its residual energy left over from a traumatic incident. I don't think anyone died in the crash even if there was an impact," she said.

"What makes you think there was not a crash?" I asked curiously.

"Because you didn't actually see or feel the impact of the crash. If you had seen the actual impact then you would know there was an accident. This may have been a near accident that was so traumatic that it left a psychic imprint behind."

"I guess I need to sage the car, and that should get rid of the residual energy."

"Yes, that is all you have to do." She said, and hung up.

I saged the car, and used anointing oil to bless the vehicle. After that, the visions ceased. Sometimes material items can absorb energy from a traumatic or life changing event in a person's life. Rarely do people realize that they give away or leave behind some of their energy.

THE DREAM

When those on the other side have a message for you, but cannot get through to your conscious mind, they will seek other ways of communicating with you. It seems like the only time when our minds are truly open is when we are asleep. It is then when those on the other side are able to connect with the living. That is what happened to me when I was 9 years old. It was April 1970 and I was in the 6th grade. My class was scheduled to go to outdoor school. I was excited to leave home, and have a break from the tension and stress that was my constant companion at home. The ride from the school to the camp took a little over an hour. I sat next to my best friend Alice, talking the entire trip. I could tell by the looks she kept giving me that she was seeing a side of me that she had never seen before. I was usually very introverted, and only spoke when spoken to, much of the time. I was chattering away like I didn't have a care in the world.

Once we arrived at the camp we were separated into groups of ten for each cabin. I was in woodchuck cabin along with my friend Alice. We put away our personal items, and were assigned a bunk. After unpacking and rolling out our sleeping bags we met our counselors outside and everyone went for a nature walk. All the counselors were given nature names instead of using their real names. Our two counselors were named Sunshine and Otter. They were high school seniors with a great sense of humor and knew how to relate to us. By the time we finished our walk it was time to go to the dining hall and have dinner. There was so much noise during dinner that you couldn't hear yourself think.

After dinner it was dark and someone had made several campfires. Each campfire had a couple of rows of bleachers forming a circle around the fire. We were taught camp songs and told stories about the history of the camp. By the time the campfire gathering was over it was after eight o'clock. We all returned to our cabins to get ready for bed. I finished getting ready for bed and crawled sleepily into the top bunk. I was so exhausted I could hardly keep my eyes open and fell fast asleep. Sometime during the night, I started to dream. When the dream began I was sitting on the porch of my grandparents' house talking to my grandfather.

"So, little one, how is it going at home?" he asked.

"It's always the same grandpa. I never know when mom is going to hit or yell at me. Sometimes I just wish I wasn't even born," I answered, sighing heavily.

"It's alright child, it won't last forever, and then you can leave home and get away from her. I'm sorry you have to go through this; I'm so ashamed of my daughter. That is not how she was raised. I never laid a hand on her; in fact she was spoiled rotten." He said, sadly shaking his head.

"Can't you talk to her and make her stop"? I implored.

"Sweetheart, I have tried before and it only made things worse for you. I'm afraid all I can do is to be here for you."

"That's okay grandpa, at least I can talk to you and grandma."

"I need to talk to you about that, June Ann. I won't be with you for much longer; it is almost time for me to be with God."

"No grandpa you can't leave me. Why do you have to go?" I pleaded, "It's not fair, please take me with you?"

"No, it is not your time; you need to stay and take care of your grandma for me."

I started to cry, and he reached out and hugged me to his chest. "Don't worry June bug, I'll always be there watching over you." I was confused, and still didn't understand what he was talking about, so I asked him to explain. "My physical body is not in good shape, it won't last much longer, I'm afraid. But that is okay because soon I'll be an angel and can watch over you from heaven."

The next thing I knew the dream had changed, I saw my grandfather lying in a casket and I started to cry. I was crying so hard that it woke me. Still crying I looked around the cabin. It was still dark, and I didn't want to wake anyone, so I grabbed my pillow, put it over my head and cried myself back to sleep. When I woke the next time, the sun was just coming up. I got up, got dressed and headed out to go to breakfast.

During breakfast I heard our two cabin counselors talking.

"Did you hear someone crying last night?"

"Yes, it was so loud it woke me up. I couldn't tell who it was."

"It sounded like someone's heart was breaking. I wish I knew who it was."

I didn't say anything; this was something too terrible to talk about.

As children do, over time, I almost forgot about the dream. I tried not to think about the dream, or what it meant. Then five months later my grandfather died, and a part of my childhood died with him.

My older brother and I were not allowed to go to the funeral. My mother made us sit out in the car and wait, watching our four-year-old half-brother. We were never allowed to say goodbye to him, so for me, the whole funeral was surreal. I have never forgiven my mother for not allowing us to go to the funeral. I spoke to my grandmother afterwards, privately. I told her about the dream that I had at outdoor school. I never spoke about it to my mother because I knew she would not understand.

"You did the right thing in not telling your mother. I think you are ready to start learning about your gifts, and how to use them. I wanted to wait until you were older, but you are opening up on your own, and that can be dangerous. You need to learn about the paranormal, and those on the other side, including angels and demons."

She explained to me the reason for my dream. "His soul came to you in the dream to let you know what was coming, and to help you prepare for his death. Your guides and guardians were the ones who helped his soul make the connection. This allowed him to give you his message. He wanted to let you know that he would always be there for you, even though he was gone."

Finally, I understood that he loved me so much that he wanted me to be the first to know that he was going to die. It made me feel loved and sad at the same time. I knew there was nothing I could do but wait.

"You need to know more about how your gifts work and how to control them. Your mother is afraid of her own gifts, so she shut them out. Your mother would never approve of me teaching you anything about your gifts. So to avoid problems for you, we'll have to do it when no one else is around."

"That's okay with me; will it help me to hear grandpa?"

"Yes, you'll be able to see and hear him."

"How can we do it without mom finding out?" I asked.

"You can either ride your bike or walk over here a couple of times a week. I'll tell your mother you're helping me with housework. By telling her that, it will ensure that your brother doesn't come along. After all, no one hates work more than your brother," she said, and we both started laughing. So for the next eight years, I made the 2 mile bike ride to my grandmother's house as often as my mother would allow. During those years she taught me about the history of our gifts, when to use them, and how to control them. She also taught me how to tell the good entities from the bad ones, and the knowledge I needed to protect myself.

GET OUT OF MY HEAD

In early October, I received an e-mail letting me know that the Body, Mind and Spirit expo would take place in a couple of weeks. I dismissed it because I had to work that weekend. The notice popped up again a few days later, and again I deleted the e-mail. The following week the e-mail reappeared a third time. Tuning into my guides, I heard them say, "You need to go; there is someone there who needs a message."

"Who is this person, male or female? How will I know it is the right person?"

"Don't worry you will know when you see him," she answered.

"You know I hate it when you guys get all cryptic!" I said in frustration.

"I know." She said, grinning.

"It will have to wait until Sunday, because I have to work on Saturday."

"That's all right, he'll be there." She said serenely.

Two weeks later I called Linda, my sister-in-law, and asked her if she wanted to go with me to the Body, Mind and Spirit expo that was being held in downtown Portland.

"Hey woman, do you want to go with me to the expo on Saturday? There's something that I have to do there."

"Sure what time do you want to go? I don't get off work until 9:30."

"If you come directly from work to my house we can go from there."

"Okay, I'll be there around 9:45. What do you have to do there? Is it something you have to do for God? Are you supposed to meet someone or give them a message or something?"

"Yes, I have to deliver a message, but it's not God's work. My guides were contacted by another soul who needs me to deliver a message." I said, sighing heavily.

"Better you than me," she laughed. "Who is this person you are supposed to give a message to?"

"I don't know. The only information I had was that a male spirit had a message that required a spirit medium. I don't know what the message is either. They frustrate me sometimes." I said.

"I guess we'll find out when we get there. This should be interesting, especially if you don't know if it's a vendor, or someone who's a visitor." Linda said.

"It never occurred to me that it might be a visitor."

Looking at my guide, floating above my bed I said telepathically, "You guys better say something when I find this person or I am not doing this again."

She laughed and said, "Not to worry, we won't leave you guessing, we'll let you know when you see him."

"Hey, what's going on over there, are they saying something?" she asked.

Linda arrived Saturday morning and we drove to the transit center to catch the train. We arrived shortly after they opened around 10:30 am. We bought our tickets and started wandering around, looking at every vendor booth. As I walked to each booth, I waited for my guides to say that this was the one.

"Are you getting anything yet?" Linda asked.

"No, not so much as a whisper and we're almost done with the booths. The only thing left are the readers."

We had been through the other vendor booths, and only the psychics and mediums booths remained.

"It looks like it may be one of the readers." Linda said.

"Yes, but which one? There are several men." connecting with my sister Ann I asked, "Give me a hint will you?"

"It is the young man at the back of the room. He is the one who needs the message; sit down in front of him," she urged.

I turned to my sister-in-law and said, "See the young guy at the back table?"

"You mean you have to give him a message? He's a psychic for goodness sake; can't he hear his own messages?"

I burst out laughing.

"What are you laughing at?" She asked, looking indignant.

"I was just thinking the same thing myself. I totally agree with you, but sometimes as a medium, we need validation about what we are hearing. We may want something so much that we are not sure if we are hearing the truth, or if it is just wishful thinking."

"I never thought about it, but I can see what you mean."

"They want me to go over and sit down for a reading."

"Come on let's get it over with so we can at enjoy the rest of the expo." Nudging her arm, I headed for the man's table.

"Hello, please sit down," he said, starting to shuffle a deck of Tarot cards and, laying them out on the table in front of him.

"What can I help you with?" he asked.

Internally, I asked my guides, "What is the message you have for him?" My own consciousness was pushed to the back, and another consciousness took over my body. Words were coming out of my mouth, but it was not me talking. "It is going to be alright Damion, all of your legal problems will be resolved in June. You will no longer have that problem hanging over your head; it is going to turn out in your favor."

Then the consciousness left, and there was only mine. Looking to the right, I noticed my sister-in-law looking at me strangely. I looked over at Damion, and he was just staring at me with a look of astonishment on his face.

"Tell your mom to stop doing that, the next person she jumps into might not be so nice about channeling her! Internally I said: "All you had to do was ask, you're not supposed to just jump in to someone to channel. You need to ask permission. Here comes Michael, (the Archangel), and he doesn't appear to be very happy." I could tell he was upset because usually his countenance is a pure white, but it was a fiery yellow now.

"I don't care, it was worth it to give my son the message." she said, and left.

"Well I guess I can leave now that you got the message." I said, getting up.

"Thanks for the message; I'm sorry about my mom doing that. She was always a strong person in life." He said apologetically.

"She's not strong; she's very stubborn and very pushy! She won't be doing that again because I'm under Michael's protection and he's angry. See you later" and I turned and left with my sister-in-law following behind me.

I headed for the coffee shop to get a cup of Chai tea. After we got our drinks, we sat down and I noticed that she still had that strange look on her face.

"Why are you looking at me like that?"

"Your whole face changed just before you gave him the message. It wasn't you at all. I was looking at someone else completely." she said, in awe.

Taking a deep breath, and a long drink of my tea, I told her what happened. "It wasn't me, my consciousness was pushed back and his mother's took over. It was his mother who was giving the message. That is what happens when you channel. But, she never asked permission, and she just took over and I was not prepared for it. I didn't have my shield up, and she took advantage of it. I will never go unprotected again. I really hate when that happens; it leaves me feeling violated!"

"I don't blame you; I wouldn't want someone to do that to me either. Let's forget about it and enjoy the expo. I'm sure you have your protection up now, so we won't have to worry about that again."

"Yes you can be sure of that, no more surprises. You're right; let's not let one pushy old woman ruin our outing."

We finished our drinks, returned to the expo and enjoyed the rest of our girl's day out. After that incident, I never went out without my protection in place.

VISUAL WARNING

Visions are defined as something seen in a dream or trance: an image or series of images often interpreted as having religious, revelatory, or prophetic significance. They are also frequently called waking dreams.

Spirit guides and guardians can give you visions of things to come. Sometimes the vision contains a warning, at other times it is a vision of hope and things to come. Waking visions are more common than people think. They tend to occur when you are in a relaxed state of mind. When they occur, your perception of time is altered. These visions usually last only a few minutes or even seconds. When they pass you are left with a feeling of disorientation. You have the sense that a lot of time has passed, when in reality, only mere seconds have elapsed.

This has happened to me on several occasions. The most memorable of these was my motorcycle accident in 1988.

It was early Saturday morning, and I was watching cartoon shows. I love the old Looney Tunes cartoons, and Wiley Coyote was just about to get smashed when the screen disappeared. In its place, I was seeing through the eyes of a person riding a motorcycle. I could not see the type of bike, only the handlebars and the road ahead. I was making a left hand turn on a green light when I saw a flash in my mirror. A car was headed straight for me from the right, and was not stopping. I didn't see, but felt the impact, then blackness and the vision stopped. My two younger brothers also rode at that time, so I assumed that the warning was for them. My brothers were both reckless drivers, and I have always been a very cautious rider. I should have known that the warning was for me, but I misinterpreted the warning, and one week later the vision was fulfilled.

It was a beautiful fall day, perfect for riding one of my motorcycles. I had just repossessed my older bike, a 1979 Suzuki GL 425 from the person who had made no payments for 6 months on it. I had been dating my future husband for only a few months when the accident happened. He had expressed an interest in learning how to ride so I thought that I would teach him on the Suzuki. I had just taken the bike out for a spin to make sure it was in good running condition. I decided at the last minute to ride it out to show him the bike he would be learning on. It was the perfect fall day, not a cloud in the sky and the sun was warm on my body.

The light in the left turn lane ahead of me had just turned green so I started my turn. Just as I entered the intersection I saw a flash of an oncoming car out of the corner or my eye. Turning my head I had just enough time to see the oncoming vehicle. Instinct took over and I remembered to push myself off the opposite side of the bike. I never made it completely off of the bike. I managed to get my right leg over the seat before the car hit me. The force of the impact sent me flying off the bike and across the road. My body landed about 100 feet from the crash site. I wasn't wearing a helmet, and I hit my head on impact. At that moment I felt my soul leaving my body.

I was bathed in a soft, white light. It felt warm and loving. In the distance I could see two people walking towards me. As they drew closer, I could make out my grandma and grandpa smiling at me. I ran toward them hugging each of them tightly.

"Grandma, grandpa how can you be here, you're dead?" I asked.

"You can see us because you just died." Grandma said.

"It is not your time; you are having this experience because you need validation about a few things. You will need to return to your body; you have so much more to do. You have a long life a head of you, another 65 years." my grandpa said.

I thought for a moment, remembering my short life, and knew instinctively that they were right.

"Yes, somehow I know you are right, I do need to return. There is so much more that I need to do in this lifetime."

"You have a job to do for God, but that won't start for a couple of more years." Grandma informed me.

"You're going to have a son, June Ann, and I'll be there to watch over him for you." grandpa told me smiling.

"Wow, a son, I think I'll name him after you grandpa." I told him with a big smile.

I noticed another figure hovering in the background. "Who's that grandma?" I asked nodding towards the figure.

"That's Michael; he was your son in your lifetime in the 1800's. He will come back again as your son in this lifetime."

Michael came over to me, took my hand and said, "Come with me child, I need to show you something."

He led me over to a white wall with a large bay window in it.

Pointing to the window he asked, "What do you see child?"

Looking out the window I could see the earth and everyone in it. Looking closer I noticed that everyone had a tiny, delicate thread extending from their head to where we were.

"What is that thread coming out of their heads?" I asked Michael.

"That is the soul connection. Everyone has this connection, but only about 20 percent of them ever use it."

"Let me ask you something, if this is heaven, does hell really exist?"

Leaving the window Michael walked away from me a few feet, and then motioned for me to follow him. He pointed at what I thought was a floor made of white, fluffy clouds. He waved his hand over a spot in front of him. Suddenly, the spot opened up and I could see nothing but blackness. It looked like a thick, black tar-like substance. A piercing scream filled my head, and I could feel the evil emanating from it. Waving his arm over the spot again, the opening closed.

"I guess that answered my question about hell."

"It's time for you to return to your body." He said.

"How do I do that?"

"Just think about returning to your body, and it will happen. This only works if you are meant to go back. If this was meant to be the end of your life, you wouldn't be able to return to your body."

I gave both of my grandparents another big hug, then thought about returning to my body. Suddenly, I woke up lying on the pavement. A police officer was leaning over me, looking worried. I must have been gone for a couple of minutes, but it seemed like hours on the other side.

"How do you feel?" the police officer asked.

"I'm fine, why?"

"You didn't have a pulse when I checked you the first time."

"Yes, I know, I was dead." I said with a sense of unreality.

Because of a concussion, I have no memory of the actual accident; and for a year after the accident, I had short term memory loss. It's funny, but the one thing that I didn't forget was my visit with my grandparents. I've never told anyone about dying, until I decided to write my books.

DEMON IN THE MIRROR

It was early June, and I was at home cleaning house, when one of my guardians came to me. "June Ann, someone is coming back into your life that you haven't seen in many years."

"Will the person be male or female?" I asked telepathically.

"Female, her name starts with a 'J'."

"I can't think of anyone at the moment. Is she a person that I want to see again?"

"Yes and no, I would say."

"You are being awfully cryptic about this person. I am not going to worry about it now; I'll deal with it when it comes up." I said, shrugging.

A few weeks went by with no word from my guides about the person with the 'J' name. Then one day I got a call from my younger brother Lee, he said he had run into an old friend of mine. It was the woman with the 'J' name. I'll call her Jenna.

"Hey, I ran into Jenna the other day, and she's staying at mom's old house. She's having a problem with what sounds like a haunting."

"What type of haunting are we talking about, that house has never been haunted. If there's something there, it is because she brought it with her." I had a sick feeling in the pit of my stomach. I grew up in that house and I was never happy there. It held a lot of painful and depressing memories for me. I am sure that there is plenty of psychic residual from when I lived there, to attract a negative. My mother had a habit of beating her children if we did something wrong. She would grab anything she could get her hands on to beat us with. It didn't matter whether it was a board, belt, or her fist, as long as it was handy.

"I didn't know there were different types of haunting; I thought a haunting was a haunting. She said there was something making noises in the house. Can you call and talk to Jenna about it?" My brother wanted to know. "I stopped by the other day and I could swear that I saw something black dart across the backyard, it gave me the creeps. She wants to move out of the house as soon as she can."

"I know it's negative, I can sense it. It's more than just your usual run-of-the mill negative entity. Moving won't help her; it's actually attached to her. It has integrated itself into the walls of the house. I'm not relishing the thought of calling her. Give me her number, and I'll call her once I've spoken with God to see what she needs to do. It may not be today, but it will be soon. How long has she been dealing with this?"

"She told me that it has been going on for over 8 years. She says they hear scratching and clawing in the walls, growling noises and objects are being moved. I know it's negative, but what do you think it is? Could it be a shadow person?"

"No, it's more than that I'm afraid. Hold on a minute, Ann has something to tell me about what's going on." My sister Ann, one of my guides, began talking to me telepathically.

"It's a demon June Ann, and it needs to be removed. She invited it in by using an Ouija board, and it's been attached to her ever since. Fortunately for her, the demon has integrated itself into the house, so it will be easier to remove. It if had been attached to her physically, it would be very hard to remove. You would have had to do an exorcism on her personally, but because it was stupid enough to reside in the house, it makes it easier to remove. God says to tell her to leave the house for 3 days, and not to return until the morning of the fourth."

"Okay, I'll have Lee tell her what to do."

"Are you still there?" My brother asked. "Hello, talk to me, what's she saying?"

Turning my attention back to the phone, I let him know what he needed to tell Jenna.

"God is sending Archangels in to deal with the demon."

"You were right; it is something more than a regular, negative entity. I'm glad I never went into the house. I had a bad feeling about it. Okay, I'll tell her what to do. But, will you call her?   This whole situation gives me the creeps."

"You have to call Jenna, tell her I said to leave the house *now,* for 3 days, and not to return until the fourth day, nothing more than that."

"But why can't I tell her what you said about the removal?" he asked.

"Because, if you tell her, the entity will know; then it will reattach itself to her, and she'll need to have an exorcism performed. While it's attached to the house, the Archangels can remove it. It won't go willingly, so there will be a big fight. Usually, they cast it back into hell. It is unusual for a demon to travel by itself, they are like coyotes, and travel in packs. You say you only saw one figure?"

"Yeah, that's the only one I saw. Jenna said that sometimes, she thinks there might be more than one, but she's not sure."

"There has to be at least one more entity there, and it is hiding for some reason. Obviously, the entity in the house is stronger, and more dominant than the other," I reasoned out loud. "I'm not about to find out, that's for sure! I'll let her know what to do, and I'll give you a call after she returns to the house."

"Okay, let her know I'll call her after this is done." I hung up the phone, deep in thought. On the fourth day, Jenna returned to the house. She told my brother the house looked like a tornado had gone through it, but it felt lighter, and all the bad feelings were gone. A few days after the cleansing, of Jenna began packing to move.

I called her a couple of days after the removal of the demon. "How is it going, does the house feel better?"

"Yes, it feels much better, but I still want to move. After what I've been through here, I just want to get away from the memories, and start fresh. Is there any way you can help me? Do you know anyone who has a truck?"

"I have a truck, but I have to work, so it has to be on the weekend. I can ask my older brother Steven if he'll help us. He's staying with me for awhile. We can always use another pair of strong hands."

"Thanks, I'll have everything ready to go when you come on Saturday." She assured me, hanging up.

We arrived the following Saturday to move her things. I could feel that the entity had been removed from the house, but I still felt uneasy near the garage. Once we had finished emptying the house, my brother said to me, "I left a few things in the garage, and I want to take them back to the house with me."

As soon as he opened the garage door, I felt a negative presence. God may have cleaned out the house, but there was still a presence in the garage which was separate from the house. My brother was already inside the garage, and as I entered, he picked up a large mirror.

"This is my mirror, and I want to bring it back with me. I had a lot of things here, and now there are only a couple of things left. I want to know what mom did with my stuff." He turned and looked at me with pure hate in his eyes.

It was then I knew that the other demon was residing within the mirror. It was influencing my brother, feeding off of his anger, and hatred for our mother. "You can't take that mirror to my house."

"Why can't I, it's mine!" he said angrily.

"Because there is a demon trapped inside of it, and I don't want it near my home. It is already using your anger and hate to strengthen itself." I told him quietly.

He looked at me for a moment, and then said, "If there is a demon trapped in it, I'm going get rid of it."

Suddenly, we both heard a growl that seemed to emanate from the mirror. Then a deep sinister voice said, "No, you are not."

I heard my brother say, "Oh yeah, let's see how you survive this!"

As I watched in horror, I saw him lift the mirror over his head, his intentions were clear. He was going to smash the mirror which would release the demon. This was just what the demon wanted. Knowing that I could not stop him, I called on the Archangel Michael.

In a split second, Michael, the Archangel appeared, just as my brother threw the mirror into the bed of the pickup. As it shattered, the demon was released, and Michael grabbed it sending the demon back where it belonged.

"Listen, don't ever do that again; shattering the mirror was the worst thing you could do. You did exactly what the demon wanted you to do, he wanted you to set him free." I said to him angrily. "If I hadn't asked for Michael's intervention you could have had it attached to you!"

Although the demon was removed, my brother was never the same. He began to drink heavily, and his anger was always present. As the weeks went by, he became more withdrawn, and hostile towards everyone, including God. He had always been a weak person, who was easily influenced. Encountering the demon had a negative influence over him.

I came home one day, and went into the room where he stayed in my house. The room was a mess, and I found evidence that he had been trying to burn my new French doors with a lighter. There was also residue of what appeared to be cocaine on the table.

I could no longer let him stay in my home for fear he would do something to endanger my family. While he was at work that day, I boxed up his things, and placed them in the driveway. When he returned home, I confronted him with what I had found.

"Hey, what are my things doing out here?" he demanded angrily.

"Why did you try to burn my French doors?" I asked.

"What are you talking about?"

"I'm talking about the burn marks on the upper casing. I also found what looks like cocaine residue, and you are drinking too much. There are alcohol bottles everywhere. Your anger and attitude are palpable. You've been affected by the demon's presence at mom's house." Holding out my hand I said, "Give me my keys, you need to leave and not return."

"You are crazy, that thing didn't influence me, and I am immune to it. Where am I supposed to go? How do I know that you are not keeping some of my things? I want to come in and check." He said belligerently.

"No, now start loading, and don't come back."
As I watched him pack and leave I could feel the influence of the dark presence. He had dealt with the demon without any protection. He thought that he could not be influenced by it, but he was wrong.

Once the active demon was removed by God, the physical manifestations ceased, but the darkness in the form of depression and anxiety haunted Jenna. Once you have been touched by the darkness, you will forever be a target. To this day she is still haunted by the memory of the demonic attachment.

A WORD OF WARNING

Ghosts, spirits and angels can warn you of impending danger. They can communicate this in different ways. You may have a prophetic dream, a sick feeling in the pit of your stomach, a sense of foreboding, a vision, a whisper in your ear or they may even appear to you. This has happened to me many times, but one of the most memorable is the warning I received from my grandmother.

It was 1984, and I was working for a cardiology clinic at the time. It was a busy morning and I decided that I needed a cup of coffee to get me through the rest of the day. I went into the break room and poured a cup of strong, black coffee. As I was about to put the sugar in, I heard someone say my name.

"June Ann."

I turned to look behind me since the voice seemed to come from that direction. There was no one in the room, and the door was shut. I stopped for a moment and replayed the voice in my head. The tone sounded like my grandmothers voice, and it sounded urgent. My grandmother had been dead for over five years, but I have always felt her presence beside me.

"Grandma is that you" I asked telepathically.

"Yes, you need to be very careful on your drive home tonight."

"Why, what is going to happen, will there be an accident?"

"It is against the rules for me to say any more than this."

"Thank you for the warning, I promise to be careful."

I finished preparing my coffee and sat down for a moment to go over what my grandmother said. I did not know if the warning was meant for that day, or if she was just warning me to be a more careful driver. Knowing I wouldn't receive any more information, I took my coffee back to my desk and thought nothing more of it until I was getting off work.

Coming out of the building, I thought how much I hated driving home in the dark. Getting into my car, I paused for a moment before starting it. I decided that I would treat the warning like it was meant for today's drive home. Starting the car I heard my grandmother again, "Remember to drive carefully June Ann."

I drove very carefully on the way home. I was halfway there when I caught a movement out of the corner of my eye. I had just enough time to register that it was a car with no lights on as it pulled out directly in front of me. Slamming on the breaks I narrowly missed the speeding car. I sat for a moment shaking, and trying to catch my breath. The sound of a car horn blaring behind me jerked me out of my revere. Putting the car in gear, I headed towards home.

Once home, I sat down for a few minutes to recover, and opened my mind to thank my grandmother for her warning. I received a soft "you're welcome" in response. This was the first of many times my grandmother would warn me of impending danger.

DARK PORTAL

There are different types of portals into the spiritual world. Most portals allow souls who have recently left the physical body to ascend into the afterlife. There are the portals that swing both ways. These portals allow souls to come and go, in visitation to the physical world. Then there are the dark portals that someone may have opened using the dark arts, or where the veil between the two worlds has worn thin. I have encountered all three types of portals, and needless to say, the dark ones are not my favorite. Whenever found, these portals should be closed, if possible. I have only closed a few of them; here is what happened with my first encounter with a dark portal.

I was sitting in my home office, working on the editing of my first book when the phone rang, startling me. Sighing, I picked up the phone and answered it.

"Hello..?"

"Hey it's me, you know I moved into my house don't you?" Julie asked

"You told me you were going to be moving to your new place in about a month. Are you already moved in?"

"Yeah, I've been living here for a couple of weeks, and let me tell you there are some weird things going on over here."

"What kind of weird things are you talking about?"

"I've been having weird dreams, and it feels creepy here."

"Did you sage and salt the place before you moved in?"

"I did the smudging with the sage, but it doesn't seem to do much good. It still feels creepy, and today I think I saw a shadowy figure. Can you come over and see if you pick up on anything?"

"I can't come right now, but I'll come over this weekend and see what I can feel. In the meantime you'll need to smudge every day, and ask for God's protection."

"Okay, but if something worse happens, I'm leaving this house until you get here!"

"Alright, let me know if something else happens, and go to your mom's if you feel unsafe."

Hanging up the phone, I got an image of a swirling vortex of dark energy. I could see dark entities coming out of it. 'Great, just great,' I thought, 'that is just what I need to make my day complete, a dark portal.'

I tried to call her back, but her cell phone was not answering, so I left her a message. "Hey it's me, I think you need to go and spend the rest of the week at your mom's place. I'll pick you up there Saturday morning around eleven." I hung up the phone, hoping she would get the message later that day.

The week seemed to fly by, and suddenly it was Saturday. I spent the early part of the morning preparing for what was waiting for me. First, I rid myself of negative energy, and then I brought the light of God, Jesus and the Holy Spirit to fill, and surround me. I connected with God, and asked Him to send Raphael and Gabriel with me to show me how to close the portal. I instantly felt their presence and heard them say they were with me. I started packing the things I thought I would need: holy water, sage, black salt and anointing oil in a small bag. Driving over to Julie's mother's house I heard the Archangels discussing the upcoming event.

"I'm glad God chose us to get rid of the dark opening." Gabriel said.

"Yes, it has been a while since I closed one of these; I think I might be a little rusty." Raphael said.

Gabriel laughed, and said, "Well I'm sure you'll lose your sense of being rusty once we get there."

"Yes, you are probably right. It will be like old times, you and me together again, against the darkness. It is just what I need to hone my skills." He said, winking at me in the rear view mirror.

"I really don't know about you two, I think you're going to have way too much fun helping me with this!"

I could see them exchanging a knowing look and knew that whatever they were up to it meant trouble for someone. I was just hoping that it wouldn't be me. "You guys need to be quiet; I can see Julie is outside waiting for me."

"Why should we be quiet, you know she can't hear us. Sometimes, you forget that." Raphael said with a smile.

"I agree if you wouldn't talk to us out loud no one would even know we're here or think you're crazy for that matter." Gabriel said with a smile, and they both burst out laughing.

"Oh be quiet you two, you distract me." I said telepathically.

I slowed the car down to a stop, and Julie got in.

"I got your message." She said smiling.

"Do you know that you have a dark portal in your house?" I asked.

"Son of a sea biscuit, that's why sometimes I see things out of the corner of my eye and feel weird. What can we do about it? Do I have to move or can we get rid of it?"

"We, is right, I've brought a couple of helpers with me to make sure we get it sealed."

"Archangels are here? Which ones? Is it Michael, tell me it's Michael!" she said eagerly.

"Gabriel, how do you like that? What are we, chopped liver?" Raphael complained.

"Yeah, how come he gets all the glory, and we get all the work?"

"Alright you two, you know I love to have you with me in any kind of fight, now stop complaining." I said telepathically.

"No it's not Michael, its Gabriel and Raphael, and I'm glad they're here." I said glancing in the rear view mirror.

"That is great, double the help." Turning towards the back seat she said, "Thank you for coming guys."

"They both said 'you're welcome'."

As we made our way toward her house, the feeling of uneasiness grew stronger. The house was a mother-in-law house. It was situated in the back of the property. Pulling up in the driveway we had to walk through the backyard of the big house to get to the smaller one.

Julie got out of the car, while I sat for a minute gathering my thoughts and reinforcing my protective shield.

Julie came around to my side of the car and asked, "Is anything wrong?"

"No, there is nothing wrong, I just needed to make sure that I reinforced my protective shield. Gabriel and Raphael said that they need to explain to me what the plan is."

"Okay, no problem, I'll wait by the gate."

"Alright, what is the plan of action?"

"First we need to find the portal, I know it's in the house but we need to find the exact location." Gabriel said.

"Wait a minute; let me see if I can sense where the portal is." Closing my eyes I focused on the building. I could see a white closet and could feel the coldness emanating from it.

I looked over to where Julie was waiting, and asked, "Is there a closet on this side of the house?"

"Yes, it's right by the door, why?

"I think the portal is in the closet."

"That makes sense; it is always cold around the closet."

"Now we know where the portal is located, how do we close it for good?" I asked.

"Now that we know where it is located, we can close, and destroy it. But, first we need to make sure that there are no other negatives running around loose on the property. We need you to tell us if you sense anything. If you do, let Gabriel know, and the two of you drive them towards the portal." Raphael stated.

"Before we begin, June Ann, you will have to lay down a wide perimeter of black salt around the property, sealing it so the dark ones cannot get out. Don't worry, we'll be here if you need us but we'll have to stay clear or they'll know something is up. Once the property is sealed then they can't escape. In order to drive them toward the portal you will have to move so that they are always in front of you. You will need to spread the black salt in a wide arc so that the dark ones will have to retreat to the house. Make sure you invoke the protection of Jesus Christ as you spread the salt." Gabriel instructed.

"Okay guys let's get moving, I want to get this over with. What should we do with Julie?" I asked.

"Gabriel you go to the right, and I'll go to the left. As for Julie, you keep her with you, preferably behind you so she can't cause a problem or get hurt." said Raphael.

"Julie, they want you to stay behind me while they do what they have to do. They don't want you to be hurt or to interfere with what we are going to do."

"Okay, that's fine." She said unhappily. I knew that she wanted to be right in the thick of things, but I also knew she was vulnerable, and not strong enough to deal with the darkness. "Don't worry; there will be plenty of other chances for the warrior in you to do battle with the darkness. You are not strong enough right now to take an active part in this, but like me, you can learn from what happens."

"You are right, but it doesn't help me feel any better."

"Are you going to talk all day, or are we going to do this?" Gabriel wanted to know. I could tell he was anxious to get the portal sealed.

"Let's do it then." Turning, I handed Julie a small bag with some black salt in it. "If you see anything you think is negative, say a prayer, and toss black salt at it. Now I'm going to go in first and you follow right behind me."

"Let's get to it!" Julie said, squaring her shoulders.

I led the way through the gate, and started across the back yard, laying down a line of salt. I could sense the portal, but no active entities. I came within a couple of feet of the house, and began to lay down a circle of blessed black salt around it. After completing the circle, I let Gabriel and Raphael know the outside was clear.

When I opened the house door and stepped inside, I felt the full force of the dark portal. I could feel the Archangels beside me. I pulled the sage wand and lighter from my pocket and lit the wand. Moving to the back of the house I started cleansing the house using the sage to smudge the house.

"I ask in the name of Jesus Christ that any and all negative energy leave this house." I repeated as I fanned the smoke from the sage throughout the house. When I finished we all stood in front of the closet door.

"When you are ready, June Ann, just open the door and watch the fun begin. Make sure that you repeat everything we say." Gabriel said seriously.

Taking a deep breath and saying a brief prayer, I quickly opened the door. Once open, I could see a swirling mass that looked like a miniature tornado, only pitch black. A blast of piercingly cold air hit my body, making me shiver.

Raphael spread his wings, and moved to the right of the swirling mass, and Gabriel took up position on the left side of it. Standing over the portal they spread their arms wide over it saying "By the power, and in the name of the most-high God and Jesus Christ, I command this portal to close. I seal this portal and return it to the darkness from whence it came."

As I watched, the funnel like vortex started to close, and a piercing screech filled my ears.

"What is that horrible sound?" I asked Gabriel covering my ears with my hands.

He smiled at me and said, "That is the sound of the dark ones cries of pain as the vortex collapse's around them and is sealed. There will be a lot more of that as we shrink down the portal and return it to the darkness where it came from."

"What is it, what is happening, and why are you covering your ears?" Julie wanted to know.

"The demons are screeching, and it hurts my ears." I shouted.

"I'm glad I can't hear them."

As the portal began to shrink in size, the screeching got louder. Finally, it was sealed and sent back into the darkness, never to be reopened again.

"Wow, what a nasty job, I'm glad it's over." I said with feeling.

"Yes, I am glad that is over with as well. I may not have been able to hear it, but I could feel its power." Julie said.

Gabriel and Raphael exchanged a secretive look. "What is it you are not telling me? Come on you two, out with it."

Raphael looked at me solemnly and said, "This is the first of many such portals. In mortal form, we would be unable to close it by ourselves. There are two types of dark portals. The first is one created by man, when he opens a doorway using the dark arts. That type of doorway can be closed by another mortal. However, this type of portal was created by the dark ones, and needed heavenly intervention to close, and to send it back where it came from. As a mortal, even with your abilities, you could only seal it temporarily. If you do place a temporary seal on it, you will need to call on one of us to finish the job." Turning to Julie, I repeated what they had told me.

"How can you tell the difference between a man-made portal, and a portal made by the darkness?" Julie wanted to know.

"Yes, how do you tell which one it is?" I asked.

"You can tell by the power that emanates from it. You felt the power of this one, June Ann, do you think you will ever forget it?" Gabriel asked with a smile.

"I see what you mean; it's not something I'm likely to forget in a hurry."

Looking at Julie, I gave her Gabriel's response.

"Yes, this thing had a lot of power behind it, it is not something I'm likely to forget either." Julie said, shivering slightly. "What can I do if I come across one of these by myself?"

Gabriel and Raphael said in unison, "Pray, and surround yourself with the light of God, and run, do not walk, to the nearest exit. You were lucky this time, this was only a small portal, not a big one, but it was enough to draw several negatives to it."

I repeated their response and she said, "If this was a small one, I would hate to see what a big one can do!"

"Gabriel, you said that it draws negatives to it. Are they actually drawn into the portal, or is it more like an open invitation?" I asked curiously.

"The dark ones are attracted to it, like a moth to a flame. It acts like a short cut between your plane of existence, and theirs. Unfortunately, it is not all that uncommon, as the darkness tries to push back the light."

"Most mortals do not have the ability to deal with these portals. The reason is that most do not have the power of the white light within them, or the faith to withstand the power of the portal, let alone the entities that dwell within it." Raphael informed me.

"But you have both white light and faith, and you have us to back you up. It takes an Archangel power to be able to close these dark portals for good." Gabriel said, giving Raphael a secretive look.

"What was that look all about? What are you two hiding?"

"Child, it is not for you to know at this time, in time, all will be revealed unto you." Said a voice from somewhere above me."

"I get it, it's on a need-to-know basis and I don't need to know right now." I said in exasperation.

"Yes, it is time we were going June Ann, we have many other things that need attention." Raphael said, and they disappeared.

I turned to Julie, "They are gone, and just as the conversation was getting interesting. Oh well, what can you do, they'll be back to check on you and make sure you're okay."

We spoke for a few more minutes, and then I left her to finish settling in for the afternoon, promising to call her in a few days to see how she was doing.

This was my first experience with dark portals, but not my last.

Connect with Me Online:

MysticConnections.org

My Blog

Facebook

Twitter

A Mediums guide on facebook

OTHER BOOKS BY THIS AUTHOR

A Mediums Guide to the Paranormal

Paranormal Encounters (book 1 in the series)

Petal's Golden Wings

All books are available on Amazon.com, Smashwords.com, Kobo.com, and Kindle.com also anywhere eBooks are sold.

CPSIA information can be obtained
at www.ICGtesting.com
Printed in the USA
FSOW01n0243090316
17674FS

9 780692 386187